Writing letters in English

Writing letters in English
a practical guide

Tim Hodlin
Sue Hodlin

Oxford University Press 1979

Oxford University Press, Walton Street, Oxford OX2 6DP

Oxford London Glasgow New York Toronto
Melbourne Wellington Kuala Lumpur Singapore
Jakarta Hong Kong Tokyo Delhi Bombay Calcutta
Madras Karachi Nairobi Dar Es Salaam Cape Town

ISBN 0 19 432215 7

Illustrations by: Cherry Denman

Filmset by Filmtype Services Limited, Scarborough
and printed in Great Britain by
Lowe and Brydone Printers Ltd., Thetford, Norfolk.

Introduction

You can find everything you need to know about writing simple letters in this book.

If you have a particular problem, writing for a visa for example, you can check the contents list and see an example. It's better to go through the book carefully though and do the practice material as it comes. You will soon find that writing a clear simple letter comes naturally to you.

Write as many real letters as you can, and compare the letters you receive with the examples in the appropriate chapter. They won't look exactly the same, but try and find parts which follow the patterns which you have learnt.

When you write a letter, check each sentence. Ask yourself, "Does it make sense?", and "Have I written what I want to say?".

The book concentrates on real needs, met by foreigners in Great Britain and abroad. You will learn how to write, how to understand letters, how to apply for jobs and places at college, and how to complain in clear English!

Most of all, we hope that you will enjoy the book and use it to help your English. You will be able to stay in touch with your English and foreign friends and *use* the language even when you have no-one to talk to.

Make your letters look nice. Even if you still make some mistakes, people will be more tolerant of these in a letter which is attractively set-out and well written or well typed.

Contents

15, Haverfield Gdns.,
Richmond,
Surrey.
2/4/79

Dear Jane,

Thank you for your Christmas card. It was very pretty.

Did you have a nice Christmas? I'm sorry I haven't written before but the family was very busy at Christmas, and I have been studying for my exams.

How are you? What did you do in the holidays?

Give my love to all the family.

Love,

Susie

Here is a letter from one friend to another.
The best letters are written on unlined paper, like this one.

This is no good: and neither is this:

Use plain, clean, unlined paper.

1 The Address and the Date

15, Haverfield Gdns,
Richmond,
Surrey.

2/4/79

The Address
Look at the top right-hand corner of the letter.
The address tells you where the letter comes from.
Never write your name in this place.

15, Haverfield Gdns,
Richmond,
Surrey.

There is a space between the
address and the edge of the paper. It
looks good.

Every letter must show where it has come from.

the number of the house ⟶ 15, Haverfield Gdns
and the name of the street

the name of the town ⟶ Richmond

the name of the county ⟶ Surrey

the name of the country (you ⟶ England
only write this if your letter
is going to another country).

In England all houses have a number and every street has a name. This is how to write the address inside your letter.

First, write the number of the house.
Examples: 12 20 53 96 143

Next, write the name of the street.
Examples: Cambridge Street, Rosemont Road, Twyford Avenue, Homepark Road, Lunesdale Drive.

Practice 1 Now write any of the numbers in the examples above and then write any of the street names above after each number.
Do it like this: 53 Rosemont Road. Don't forget there is a comma , after the street name.
You may sometimes see a comma , after the number of the house. This is also correct.
Sometimes houses are divided into flats or apartments.
Examples:
Top flat
Flat 4
Flat 2
Flat 2B
Flat

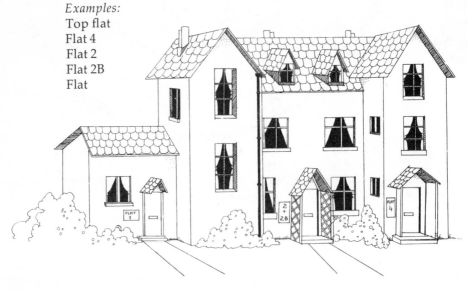

Practice 2 Now write three addresses with a flat number and the house and street underneath it. Choose a flat number from the examples.

Do it like this:

Flat 2B,
53 Rosemont Road,

Sometimes a house only has a name.
Examples: Daffodil Cottage, New Oak Cottage, Galegarth.

Often words like 'street' or 'road' are abbreviated (made shorter).
Examples: Street St.

Here is a list.

Street	St.	Terrace	Terr.	Place	Pl.
Road	Rd.	Way		Grove	
Square	Sq.	Close		Drive	
Avenue	Ave.	Lane		Court	Ct.
Crescent	Cres.	Mews		Gardens	Gdns.

Next you write the name of the village or town, or part of the town.
Examples: Marlow, Ware, Saltash, Aberdeen, Carnforth.

Practice 3   Look at the five numbers and street names you wrote in *Practice 1*.
Abbreviate the words like 'street' or 'road' if possible.
Add one of the names of a town in the examples.
Do it like this: 53 Rosemont Rd.,
               Marlow,

Counties and Postcodes

The last part of the address is the county and a postcode. Americans call this a zip code. Britain is divided into smaller parts called counties.

Here is a list of the counties in England and Wales.

The Post Office does not recommend a short form for all the counties. Only use a short form if it is in the list, or if it is already on the address you are writing to.

ENGLAND:

Avon		Hertfordshire	Herts.
Bedfordshire	Beds.	Humberside	
Berkshire	Berks.	Isle of Wight	
Buckinghamshire	Bucks.	Kent	
Cambridgeshire	Cambs.	Lancashire	Lancs.
Cheshire		Leicestershire	Leics.
Cleveland		Lincolnshire	Lincs.
County Durham	Co. Durham	Merseyside	
Cornwall (and Isles		Middlesex	Midd'x.
of Scilly County)		West Midlands	W. Midlands
Cumbria		Norfolk	
Derbyshire		Northamptonshire	Northants.
Devon		Northumberland	
Dorset		Nottinghamshire	Notts.
Essex		Oxfordshire	Oxon.
Gloucestershire	Glos.	Salop	
Greater Manchester		Somerset	
Greater London		Staffordshire	Staffs.
Hampshire	Hants.	Suffolk	
Hereford and		Surrey	
Worcester		West Sussex	W. Sussex

East Sussex	E. Sussex	North Yorkshire	N. Yorkshire
Tyne and Wear		South Yorkshire	S. Yorkshire
Warwickshire		West Yorkshire	W. Yorkshire
Wiltshire	Wilts.		

WALES:

Clwyd		South Glamorgan	S. Glamorgan
Dyfed		Gwent	
Mid Glamorgan		Gwynedd	
West Glamorgan	W. Glamorgan	Powys	

There are no authorised abbreviations for any Scottish county. Simply copy carefully the address of the person to whom you are writing.

Map of English counties

If the town or city in the address is large or well-known, you do not need to add the county name as well.
Copy an address carefully if you are not sure.

Note: Middlesex is not a 'real' county, but it exists as a postal county. (It is used by the Post Office to sort letters.)

The postcode is a group of letters and numbers with a space between like this:

W3 9BD   AB9 1AA
SL7 1AA   YO7 3JT
PR3 0BH   BR1 1BB

There are no full stops between the letters. Write the postcode underneath the town, or if you do not have much space, on the same line. You will not see a postcode all the time because not every town has the machines to sort the letters in this way. It is a good idea to write the postcode, if possible, if the address is in London, the capital of England, or another big city. It helps us to know exactly where the letter is from. It is most important to write the postcode on the envelope if possible.

Most big cities are divided into geographical areas, North, South, East, and West. You may see this written after the name of the city like this:

London W.3.   (West 3 = a part of West London)
London N.W.11. (North West 11)
Glasgow S.W.2. (South West 2)

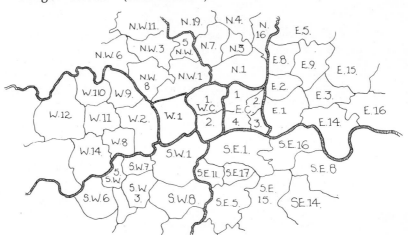

Map of London postal districts

Or you will see just the name of the district in a big city and the area it is in, like this:

Ealing W.5. There are full stops between the letters.

Practice 4   Try and complete each address you wrote in *Practice 3*.

Add a county (from the list).
Marlow is in Buckinghamshire.
Ware is in Hertfordshire.
Saltash is in Cornwall.
Aberdeen is a large town in Scotland.
Carnforth is in Lancashire.

Write each part of the address on a new line. Put a full stop at the end.

Make the address look nice.

53, Rosemont Rd,
Marlow,
Bucks

A

53, Rosemont Rd,
Marlow,
Bucks

B

Look at A and B. In example A the address slopes. In example B the address makes a straight line.
You can write the address like A or B.

Practice 5   1   Write your address on a piece of paper.
2   Write a friend's address on the other side of the paper.
3   Write the address of your school.

Don't worry if your address is not like the examples we have shown you. Write each part, (the house, the street, the town or village, the district) on a separate line.

House names, street names, and town or village names all have capital letters.

Practice 6   Here are some addresses. They are not written correctly. Can you write each address in the correct order and in the correct way?
Do it like this: Starston 14 Malt Lane IP20 9NN Norfolk

14 Malt Lane,
Starston,
Norfolk,
IP20 9NN.

Don't forget the commas and the full stops. Don't forget capital letters for street names and town and village names.

1 Marlborough House   Cornwall   Homepark Road   Saltash
2 15 Haverfield Gdns   Surrey   Kew   TW9 1JA
3 391 Clapham Road   Flat 1   SW4 7UT   London
4 Winterton   Lincs   101 Park Road
5 168 Rosendale Ave.   Dulwich   SE21 8SZ   London
6 39 Alfred Road   Surrey   Farnham

Practice 7   Read this chapter again. Now look at each problem. You must choose √ right or × wrong. Write the number of each question and put a √ or × by each one.

Ann Janes,
2, The Grove,
Hatfield,
Herts.

22, Moss Drive,
Forton,
Preston
PR3 0BH

3, Field Lane,
Twickenham,
Middx.

England,
Surrey,
Richmond.
12, Rose Court.

31, High St.
London.

16, Clarendon Court
Kew Gardens,
Surrey
TW9 1JA

The Date
The address tells us where the letter is from.
Next you must say when the letter was written. There are many ways to write the date:

8th September, 1979
8th Sept., 1979
8 September, 1979
September 8th, 1979
September 8, 1979
Sept. 8, 1979
8/9/79 (the day, the month, the year)

English people write it like this, but in the United States they write the month first, then the day, then the year. 8th September, 1979 would look like this: 9/8/79.
But, this is the most common way: 8th September, 1979

Never write 'of' in the date (8th of September) although you say 'of' if you are reading the date aloud.

There are a few dates that are different. You should learn these.
1st 21st 31st
2nd 22nd
3rd 23rd
All the others have 'th'.
Examples: 4th 6th 15th 24th 30th.

Write the date under the last line of the address. Leave a little space between the address and the date, like this:

Practice 8 **A**   Here are some short ways of writing the date. Can you write each date in full?
Example: 8/9/79 = 8th September, 1979

1   22/4/83
2   23.3.85
3   4/4/81

B   Now see if you can write the short form of these dates.
4   June 3rd, 1982
5   7th August, 1987
6   May 31st, 1979

Practice 9   Look again at *Practice 4*. Add a date to each complete address you have written.

P.S.

Write the number of the house,

the street where it is,

the town,

and the county or district.

Now you know where you are: 20, Park Avenue,
Tiverton,
Devon.

Note P.S. = Postscript. This is a sentence or sentences you can add at the end of your letter, after you have signed your name. You write a P.S. if you have forgotten to put something in your letter, or if you want to remind somebody about something. Look at the end of Chapter 3 to see how it is used in a letter. It's used here to remind you about some of the important things in the chapter.

2 The Greeting

15,
Ric
Sur

Dear Jane,

Writing to a stranger

The address tells us where the letter is from. Now you must choose the correct way to begin a letter.

You do not know his or her name. You might write a letter like this to a travel bureau, to a ministry, to an information office, or to the B.B.C.
Begin like this:

> *Dear Sir,* (man) or *Dear Sirs,*
> *Dear Madam,* (woman)

Don't forget the comma.

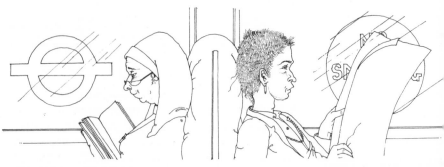

Writing to someone you know,
  or someone whose name you know,
  or someone who has written to you first.
You may not know this person very well, but if you know their name, begin like this:

Dear Mr X,
Dear Mrs X, (a married woman)
Dear Miss X, (definitely unmarried)
Dear Ms X, (a woman, either married or single. It's like Mr for men)
Dear Dr X, (this may be a medical doctor or an academic doctor)
Dear Professor X,
Dear (use their title) *X,*

Writing to someone you know quite well,
  or someone you want to be friendly with.
Begin like this:

Dear Ahmad,
Dear Jane,
Dear Michelle,

This is how English people write to their relatives, but if they write to relations of the older generation they often use titles like this:

Dear Mother,
Dear Uncle,
Dear Granny,

Writing to someone who is very close to you
Begin like this:

Dearest David,
Darling Vanya,

Here is how to write the opening of your letter and how to make it look good.

Write on the left hand side of the paper. Don't begin at the edge. Leave a little space. Use a capital letter for each word.

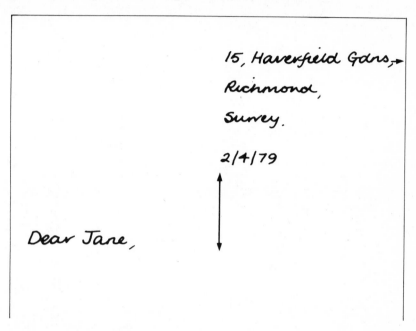

15, Haverfield Gdns,
Richmond,
Surrey.

2/4/79

Dear Jane,

Practice 10   Which opening would you use if you wrote a letter to these people? Write the answer to 1–8.
1   The London Tourist Board
2   An Employment Agency
3   Your penfriend, Isabella
4   Your boyfriend, Sebastian or your girlfriend, Marion
5   Your landlady, Pye
6   Your landlord, Pye
7   Your host, Fiddick
8   Your class friend (you choose a name)

Practice 11   Can you think about this? Imagine you are staying in England. This is where you are staying:

15, Haverfield Gardens,
Richmond,
Surrey.

It is the last day in August, 1979. You are writing to a theatre for two tickets.

You write the address and the opening of the letter. Set it out correctly. Don't write the letter yet!

P.S.

If you begin the wrong way, look what happens!

Dear Tom,

Darling Cherry,

Dear Madam,

Dear Mr X,

Always choose the right opening for the person you send your letter to.

Dear Mr Martin

3 The Ending and the Signature

It's a good idea to learn how to write the ending for your letter next. The end of your letter must match the greeting.

Writing to a stranger
In formal letters, to a stranger, to someone you know, someone whose name you know, or someone who has written to you first, this is a polite way to end:

I look forward to hearing from you.

After that, writing to a stranger,

Dear Sir or Madam,

end

Yours faithfully,

T. P. N. Shemington

Sign your formal name. Usually this means your initials and your surname. Women may show if they are Mrs or Miss if they wish. Write this in brackets ( ) before or after your name.
Example:

(Mrs) B. Dyson

If your signature is not very clear, print (write in block capitals) your name again underneath.
Example:

> *Yours faithfully,*
>
> (Miss) Carol Jarvis
>
> (Miss) CAROL JARVIS

Writing to someone you know,
   or someone whose name you know,
   or someone who has written to you first,

end like this:

> *Yours sincerely,*
>
> Timothy Shemington

You can end the letter like this too:

> *Yours,*
> or *Yours ever,*
> or *As ever,*

Just write your first name and surname. Men don't need to put their marital status; women may write it if they want to.

In friendly letters you often finish your letter with a polite wish.

It doesn't look good to talk about your English or any mistakes you think you've made.

End like this:

> *Please write soon.*
> *Write soon!*
> *I hope I'll hear from you soon.*
> *I hope you will write soon.*
> *I must end now.*

Always send best wishes or love to friends or to the family of the friend you are writing to:

> *Regards to your family.*
> *Best wishes to you and all your family.*
> *Give my love to your family.*

If your letter is to someone you see a lot, then do not end about *writing* soon; end about *seeing* them soon like this:

> *See you soon,*
> *Looking forward to seeing you next week.*
> *I'll give you a ring next week.**

Note *give you a ring = make a telephone call

Writing to someone you know quite well,
   or someone you want to be friendly with,
end:

> *Regards,*   *Best wishes,*   *Love,*
>   *Tom*   *Mathew*   *Emma*

Men do not usually use 'Love' to each other. They can use 'Regards', 'Yours', or just sign their name.

Both men and women should be careful about writing 'Love' to each other, as the meaning might be misunderstood.
Use another way to end if you are not sure.

Sign your first name or your nickname. Your nickname is the name your family or your friends call you.
Example:

Name	*Short name*	*Nickname*
Timothy	Tim	Fatty
		Timbo
Frances	Frankie/Fran	Sparrow (a bird)
	Fanny/Franny	

Writing to someone who is very close to you

End like this:

Love,   *Lots of love,*
   Susie   *Tilly*

Then you could put some kisses:

× × × × × × × ×

Use a capital letter for the first word of the ending. Don't forget the comma.

This is the best place to write the ending, in the middle of the page:

> *Best wishes,*
>
>   *Susie*

Practice 12 Look back at *Practice 10* on page 21. How would you end each letter? Choose an ending and the correct way to write your name.

Practice 13 How would you end the letter you began to ask for theatre tickets? Only write the ending. Don't write the whole letter yet!

P.S. means Postscript. This is a sentence or sentences you can add to the letter after the signature. If you have forgotten to write something in your letter, or you wish to add something else, then write it as a P.S. Keep any P.S. as short as possible.
Example:

> *See you on Saturday.*
>
>   *As ever,*
>
>   *Joe*
>
> *P.S. Don't forget to bring a bottle!*

P.S.

You will make it very difficult for anyone to answer your letter if you do this:

Best wishes,

or this:

Yours,
Sherrington

1 Make sure the end of your letter and the signature match the greeting in your letter.
2 Sign clearly who you are – man or woman.
3 Never write *'Bye-bye'* or *'Goodbye'*. These are spoken expressions only.
4 Never write 'from' after the ending of a letter.
5 Don't write the ending at the edge of the paper.

4 The Envelope

Choose an envelope which fits your letter.
Don't do this:

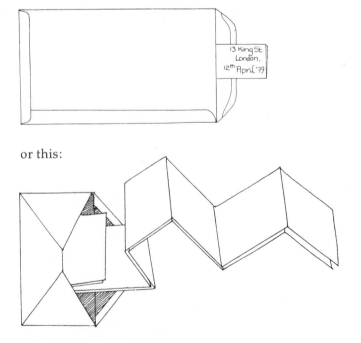

or this:

or this:

Brown (manilla) envelopes are often used for official or government letters.

Where to write the address.
Think about the stamp first. In Britain you always stick the stamp, or stamps, in the top right-hand corner. If there are a lot of stamps go along first:

and then down:

Write the address in the centre of the envelope. Where you put the first line is important. You must have enough space to write all the address.

Each address is different; just remember to make the address easy to read.

You can slope ⟍ the address or write it straight │ . This is the same as the way you write the address inside your letter. Check you are doing this correctly. Look at Chapter 1 again.

The Envelope

Practice 14 Which envelope is correctly addressed? Mark each one with a tick √ or a cross ×.

It is a good idea to write the name of the town (and the country if you are sending your letter to another country) in capital (large) letters. Look at the envelope at the beginning of this chapter.

If you are writing to someone in another country and you are using an air letter form, you will see there are spaces and lines for you to write the address and your own address on the back of the form.

If the address you are sending your letter to does not follow the pattern you have learnt, just copy the address carefully and clearly.

How to write the address
Write the address in exactly the same way as you write an address inside the letter, but add the name of the person you are sending your letter to.

The safest way is to put Mr, Mrs, Miss, or Ms

followed by their initial or initials, and the surname.
Example:

    Mr M. Bryant

If you know someone, or they like to sign their name in full like this,

then you can address the letter to

    Michael E. Bryant,
    or Mr Michael E. Bryant,.

Friends often address letters to each other like this.

Note You might see 'Esq.' (Esquire) written after a man's name, like this:

    Timothy Appleton, Esq.,

This is an old form and not in general use.

If you do not know the name of a person, or you just want to send your letter to a section or department, make it clear where you want your letter to go. You can just write the position of the person you are writing to.

Practice 15 Draw five envelopes 15cms × 10cms and write the envelopes for each of these letters.
1   You are writing to renew a visa to the Home Office, Lunar House, Wellesley Road, Croydon, CR9 2BY.
2   You are writing to your friend, Jane Fisher, 121 Addison Way, London, N.W.11.
3   You live in Iran and you are writing a letter for a subscription to the magazine BBC Modern English, Modern English Publications, 35 Shaftesbury Avenue, London W1V 7DD.
4   You are writing to a penfriend, a boy, Neuler Pecenha, 24 Thornton Road, Acton, London, W.3.
5   You are replying to a letter from Charles Carter, PhD, the Principal of the Abbey Language School, 12 Abbey Road, High Wycombe, Bucks. You do not live in England.

Sometimes you write to people, but you do not know their permanent address. You only know where they are at college or school, or where they might be staying.
In this case write: c/o (care of).

Example:

> Miss Jane Fisher,
>   c/o Abbey Language School,
>   12 Abbey Road,
>   High Wycombe,
>   Bucks.

If you think the person you are writing to has moved somewhere else, write Please Forward in the top left-hand corner of the envelope. Then the letter will be sent to him at his new address. *Example:*

PLEASE FORWARD

Charles Parton Esq.
  7 Saint Barnabas Street,
    Oxford
      Oxfordshire

P.S.

This letter is not going to arrive anywhere.

1 Choose a clean envelope.
2 Write the address in the centre of the envelope.
3 Write the name first. If there is no name, write the department or the position of the person you are sending your letter to.
4 Write the complete address. Use capital letters for the name of the town.
5 Stick the stamps on in a sensible position.

5 Enquiries and Understanding the Reply

Dear Sir,
    I would be grateful if you would send me information about English courses for foreigners in london.
    Yours sincerely
    Rankin.

Letters of enquiry are usually quite formal.
Write your own address in the usual place. It's a good idea to write the address of the place you are sending your letter to on the left-hand side, a little lower down like this:

> 20 Bushy Park Road,
> Teddington,
> Midd'x.

BBC English by Radio,
P.O. Box 76,
Bush House,
Strand,
London, WC2B 4PH.

General enquiries.

If you want information about anything, begin like this:

> *Dear Sir,*
> *I would be grateful if you would send me information*
> *about* . . . .

If you want some more details about something in the letter you are writing, begin like this:

> *Dear Sir,*
> *I would be grateful if you would send me more details*
> *about* . . . .

Note In this sentence, *'I would be grateful if* . . . . . .' either *'would'* or *'should'* may be used. Use the same form throughout your letter. You do not need to add any polite phrase at the end, because these are very short letters. Just end the letter and sign your name.

Here are some things you might want to write a letter about. You can begin them all like the examples:

> finding out about English courses
> asking about lodgings
> getting train/plane/bus timetables
> asking about entertainment/clubs/discotheques
> asking about rates and facilities for hotels
> finding out about English schools
> asking about permits/visas
> tourist information
> asking for posters/details of fan clubs/
> books/leaflets/booklets/catalogues
> asking for forms.

Remember, this is probably your first letter to someone about what you want, so . . . . . .

just say in simple English what it is you want.

Examples:

154, Horb 1/Rexingen,
Allemandstrasse 15,
West Germany

Association of Recognised
English Language Schools,
43 Russell Square,
London WCIB 5DH

Dear Sir,
      I would be grateful if you would
send me information about English classes
for foreigners in London in the summer.

            Yours faithfully,
            (Miss) Helga Spohn

9a. Anerikis Street
Athens.

The British Council,
10, Spring Gardens,   10/3/1980
LONDON S.W.1.

Dear Sir,
      I would be grateful if you would tell
me where I can obtain a copy of the handbook
'How to live in Britain'.

            Yours faithfully,
            Angela Kakas

31 rue Estienne d'Orves,
92400 VINCENNES

Alliance Française,
25, Queensberry Place,   10/3/80
LONDON S.W.7.

Dear Sir,

I would be grateful if you would send me details of any French and German clubs in London.

Yours faithfully,
Michelle Pennod.

Schonen, 12
8803, Ruschliken.

YMCA,
National Council,   10/3/80
644, Forest Road,
LONDON E.17.

Dear Sir,

I would be grateful if you would send me details about accommodation in London at student hostels.

Yours faithfully
F. Chalot.

Practice 16 You write a letter asking for information. Each number gives you the information. You write the letter. You need not practise the address again.

1 A handbook, 'How to Apply for Admission to a University': where can you get a copy?
2 Short summer courses in English language: you want addresses of schools in London.
3 You are going to go on holiday to Scotland from King's Cross station: you want train timetables.

4   You want to know how you can arrange to study at an English
    school.
5   Special exhibitions and events during Easter in Oxford.
6   A form to apply for membership of the squash club in Ealing.
7   You want to get the 'Mothercare' catalogue.
8   You want to know about the rates for a double room with all
    meals at a hotel.

Personal description and penfriends

When you write for information about some things, you include a
short personal description. This will help the person you are
writing to give you the correct information.
These are the things to write.

age	I am a 25 year-old . . . . .
	I am a 15 year-old . . . . .
nationality	I am a 25 year-old Iranian . . . . .
	I am a 15 year-old German . . . . .
sex	I am a 25 year-old Iranian man
	I am a 15 year-old German girl
education	I have finished high school/university/college
	I have completed five years of secondary school
ability	and have passed/failed my diploma/exams
interests	I am interested in music
	or stamp collecting
	or folk dancing
	I like reading
	or travelling
	or studying languages

Your letter would look like this:

154, Horb 1 / Rexingen,
Allemandstrasse 15,
West Germany

8ᵗʰ May, 1979

Dear sir,

*   I would be grateful if you would*
send me the name of an English pen-friend.
*   I am a 17 year old German girl. I have*

> *finished High School and have passed my*
> *English exam. I am interested in pop music*
> *and collecting pen friends*
>
> > *Yours faithfully*
> > *(Miss) Helga Spohn*

Practice 17 Likes and Dislikes.

Make a list of five things *you* like or are interested in. Then try and ask a friend if he likes or dislikes each thing. Put a √ or a × against each subject. Remember, TELL THE TRUTH!

Practice 18 Write a short description of yourself: age
                                              nationality
                                              sex
                                              education
                                              ability

You begin each paragraph on a new line, a little further from the edge, every time you write a new idea.

Practice 19 Use your own address and write a short letter to a magazine asking for an English pen-friend.

In some letters of enquiry you only need to give certain information about yourself. This is to make sure you receive information that is useful to you.

Example: Ahmad, a student in Iran, has been accepted as a student at a college in England. He writes a letter to the British Embassy to ask them about visa and entry requirements. He explains why he is writing.

> > > *3rd Alley, Jamshidiyeh St.,*
> > > *Niavaran,*
> > > *Tehran.*
>
> *Visa Dept.*   *May 15th 1980*
> *British Embassy,*
> *Ferdowsi Avenue,*
> *Tehran.*
>
> *Dear Sir,*
>   *I would be grateful if you would send me details*

of visa and entry requirements for Britain.
I have been accepted as a student at a college in
London from September 1980.

Yours faithfully

A. Boroumand

A. BOROUMAND

Practice 20 In each of these questions you are writing a letter to enquire about something. You only need to give some information about yourself. Choose which items you should write in each letter by ticking √ in the appropriate column:

Give details about your:

	ability	interests	plans	age	sex	nationality
1						
2						
3						
4						

1 You are writing to an agency to ask about employment as an au pair.
2 You are writing to a company to ask about holidays where you can study your special hobby and with people of your own age.
3 You are writing to an agency which runs 'swop' holidays with children from British families.
4 You are writing to ask about work permits in Britain.

Practice 21 Now write the full letter for *two* of the topics in *Practice 20*. You need not write the addresses.

If you are writing a letter to Britain from your own country and you want to be sure to receive a reply, you should enclose a Reply coupon in your letter.
You should add you are doing this at the end of your letter.
Example:

Dear Sir,
I would be grateful if you would send me a prospectus of your language school.

I am enclosing a reply coupon.

Yours faithfully,
X

Understanding the Reply

Helga is a German girl who came to England to work as an au pair. She wrote a letter to a language school to enquire about work and about studying at the school.

What do you think she wrote?

Read the reply she received and then answer the questions.

Salton Language School

25, St. John's Ave., Saltash, Cornwall
tel.: Saltash (075 55) 2546

Member of ARELS

10th May, 1979

Miss Helga Spohn,
154 Horb 1/Rexingen,
Allemandstrasse 15,
West Germany.

Dear Miss Spohn,

Thank you for your letter of 8th May and for enclosing a reply coupon.

To find au pair work, I suggest you write to:

HELP Agency,
72 High Street,
Acton,
London, W3A 6AR.

Perhaps you would like to take our July or August course before you begin work as an au pair. I enclose full details about the school. This is a small school, where we work seriously and where the teachers take a personal interest in their students.

If you decide that you would like to study here, please return the enrolment form together with a deposit of £10 as soon as possible, so that I may reserve you a place and arrange accomodation for you.

I look forward to hearing from you.

Yours sincerely,

Peter Appleton Jarvis

Peter Appleton Jarvis
Principal

Principal: P.Appleton Jarvis, B.A. (Cambridge), Cert.Ed. (Bristol)

Practice 22 **1a** What was the first thing Helga asked about?
Give a short answer.

1b Now write down the exact words Helga wrote in the opening of her letter.

2a When do you think Helga will start work as an au pair?

2b Write down the exact words Helga wrote in her letter.

3a What do you think Helga wanted to know about the language school she wrote to?

3b She began her sentence like this. Can you complete it?
'Would you ....'

4 What does Helga have to send to this school?

5 What is the last thing Helga wrote in her letter before signing her name? Begin like this:
'I am ....'

Remember, each new idea is a new paragraph.

Practice 23 Read Helga's letter. Some of the sentences in your answers to *Practice 22* will be the same.

154, Horb 1/Rexingen,
Allemandstrasse 15,
West Germany

21st May, 1979

Dear Sir,

I would be grateful if you would send me details about working as an au pair in September. I would like to take an English course in the summer.

Would you please send me any details about your school.

I am enclosing an International Reply Coupon.

Yours faithfully,
(Miss) Helga Spohn

A student from Iran, Ahmad, wrote a letter to enquire about a place to study at a Business School.
Here is the reply he received.

London Business
and
Related Studies School

121 Lonsdale Park Gardens, Fulham, London, SW6 7EE
tel.: (01) 731 8095
telegram: BUSOL LONDON

14th March, 1980

Mr. Ahmad Boroumand,
3rd Alley,
Jamshidiyeh St.,
Niavaran, Tehran,
Iran.

Dear Mr. Boroumand,

Thank you for your letter and the enclosed certificates and references, of February 22nd, and for the International Reply Coupon.

Judging by your age and qualifications, we suggest that you enrol in our 1st year Business Studies course which begins in September 1980.

If you decide to accept this offer of a place, would you please reply as soon as possible so that we may send you further details about registration.

I am enclosing a leaflet about the course, accomodation and fees which I trust you will find helpful.

Yours sincerely,

David Taylor

David Taylor
Tutor for Admissions

Practice 24 Read the letter again and answer the questions.
  1a What is the first thing Ahmad asked for in the opening of his letter? Give a short answer.
  1b Write down the exact words he would have used.
  2 Write down *your* age, nationality and qualifications.

3a What did Ahmad ask about courses? Begin, *'He asked for . . .'*
3b Now write the *exact* words Ahmad used.
4 What did he enclose in his letter?
 a
 b
 c
Begin each new idea as a new paragraph.

Practice 25 Read Ahmad's letter. Your answers to *Practice 24* should look like some of the sentences in his letter.

3rd Alley, Jamshidiyeh St.,
Niavaran,
Tehran.

January 30th 1980

London Business School,
103-105 Regent Street,
London W1.

Dear Sir,
     I would be grateful if you would send me information about Business Study courses at your school.
     I am a 22 year old Iranian man and I have a degree in Accountancy from Tehran University.
     I would be grateful for your advice about a suitable course to study, and if my application is successful, when to come to England.
     I am enclosing photocopies of my certificate and references and an International Reply Coupon.

Yours faithfully,
A Boroumand

A. BOROUMAND

Note Ahmad refers to the fact that he is a man. Remember British people do not always know if some foreign names are male or female.

Practice 26 Imagine you are writing each of these three letters.

1 You are a 22 year-old student in Economics. You have a degree. You want to study Economics at a university in Britain. You want to know if you are qualified to do this and when the course begins. You enclose photocopies of your certificates, references, and a reply coupon.

2 You are a 25 year-old Japanese student of English and you want to come to Britain as an au pair. You are writing to an agency to enquire about jobs in large towns.

3 You are an 18 year-old girl and you want to come to Britain to take a secretarial course. You have not studied typing or shorthand before and your English is not very good. You are writing to a school to ask if there are any suitable courses you could study and the dates of the courses. You also ask about finding accommodation.

Write your own address and choose a suitable address to write to each time from this list:

The Registrar,
St. Godric's Secretarial College,
14 Fitzroy Avenue,
West Hampstead,
London, N.3.

Excell Agency,
145 Gordon Road,
Acton,
London, W.3.

Admissions Officer,
The University of Lancaster,
Bailrigg,
Lancaster,
Lancs.

P.S.

Remember, writing a letter like this, you must say what you want and you must also state any special requirements.

Sometimes you must also explain who you are. The person who reads your letter cannot see you. You must make him 'see' you in your letter writing.

This letter is bad

> 154, Horb 1/Rexingen,
> West Germany.
> 5 May
>
> Dear sir,
>   I would be grateful if you would send me the address of a pen-friend.
>
>   Yours faithfully
>   A. Sept

This is why!

6 Letters of Acceptance and Refusal

> Thank you for your offer of a place on the Business Studies course. I have great pleasure in accepting the offer.

What do you need to write in a letter accepting a job, or the offer of a place at a college, and other similar letters?

Read this letter. It is from a woman who is making the offer of a job.

15, Homepark Rd.,
Ealing,
London, W.5.

Dear Helga,

Your name has been given to me by the HELP Agency, and I am writing to offer you a position as an au pair with our family for 1 year.

The family consists of myself, my small daughter Charmian who is six years of age, and a young schoolteacher who is staying with us until January.

We live in a pleasant apartment and you will share a room with the teacher until January. After that you will have a room of your own.

We live very near the park and a good school where you will be able to study English. Your duties will include looking after Charmian (she has just started ballet classes), and general light duties in the house.

I look forward to hearing from you soon.

Yours sincerely,

Evelyn Aldwich

Practice 27 Can you answer these questions about the letter?
1 How many people live at 15 Homepark Road?
2 What kind of work will Helga do?
3 Where is the apartment?
4 Will Helga have her own bedroom?

Accepting the offer of a job

First, acknowledge the letter you have received.
Begin like this:

> *Thank you for your letter. I am pleased to accept (or I have pleasure in accepting) the position of au pair with your family.*

Read the letter again. Helga will show she is being friendly by commenting (talking about) some of the things Mrs James wrote in her letter.
Example: Charmian's ballet classes, Helga could write:

> *I am sure I will get on well with your little girl because I used to go to ballet classes.*

Practice 28 Here are some things people write in letters about their family. Can you comment on them in the same way as the example?
1 'We love the theatre and music.'
2 'Suzanne has just joined a drama club and Dominic likes karate!'
3 'We like going on picnics at the weekend and exploring the countryside.'
4 'My eldest daughter likes to play tennis and volley-ball.'
5 'The children are 14, 12, and 10 and look forward to showing you round London.'
6 'I am expecting our new baby in a month.'

Helga would like to study English while she is working as an au pair.
This is how she asks.
Example:

> *I would be grateful if you would register my name at the college for English classes.*

Practice 29 Can you ask the host family to register your name for any two courses at the college. Choose two courses that interest you from this list. Remember, choose a time to study that is suitable.

Pottery – 34 weeks

Monday	10.00 – 11.00
Monday	6.30 – 9.30
Friday	2.00 – 5.00
Friday	7.00 – 9.00

Jewellery – 34 weeks

Monday	7.30 – 10.00
Wednesday	7.30 – 10.00

Squash – 10 weeks

Thursday	10.00 – 11.00
Friday	2.00 – 3.00

Art – 29 weeks

Monday	7.00 – 9.30
Tuesday	2.00 – 4.30

Handicrafts – 34 weeks

Friday	7.00 – 9.00

Yoga – 29 weeks

Monday	10.00 – 11.30
Wednesday	10.00 – 11.30
Wednesday	7.00 – 9.30
Thursday	5.00 – 6.30

Write each example separately. You cannot study everything together! You can study courses like this at many colleges. They are very cheap.

Now Helga must tell the family where and when she is arriving.

> *I will be arriving at Victoria Station on Saturday, August 15th at 15.00 hours.*

How will the family recognize Helga?

> *I have brown eyes and short brown hair. I am quite tall and a bit plump!*

Practice 30 Describe yourself. Make sure you write a description of what you are like.

I am medium height and I have long hair with a fringe.

This is something extra Helga wrote to make sure the family know who she is.

I will be carrying a copy of 'Stern' magazine.

Practice 31 You write one sentence. Say what you would carry/hold/wear.
Note To make sure the family will recognize her, Helga also adds

I am enclosing a recent photograph of myself.

The last thing to do is to end politely.
Example:

> I look forward to meeting you.
> Yours sincerely,

Practice 32 Read through the letter of acceptance that Helga wrote.

154, Horb 1/Rexingen,
Allemandstrasse 15,
West Germany
5 May

Dear Mrs Aldwich,

Thank you for your letter. I am pleased to accept the position of au pair with your family.

I am sure I will get on well with your little girl, because I used to go to ballet classes.

I would be grateful if you would register my name at the college for English classes. I would like to study in the morning when Charmian will be at school.

I will arrive at Victoria Station on Saturday August 15th at 15.00 hours. I have brown eyes and short brown hair. I am quite tall and a bit plump! I hope you will recognize me. I will also be carrying a copy of STERN magazine.

I look forward to living with you.

Yours sincerely,

Helga Spohn

Practice 33 Now go back and read this chapter again. You write the complete reply to this letter, accepting the position of au pair.

> 12, Fairlawn Ave.,
> Highgate,
> London N.6.
> 23/6/80
>
> Dear Birgitte,
>   I was given your name by the Universal Agency and I am writing to invite you to spend a year with my family in London on an au pair basis.
>   You will be given pocket money of £12.00 a week in return for general help in the house and looking after the children. The family consists of two adults and two girls (14 and 12) and a baby boy. I am sure you will enjoy the company of the girls who will help you a lot to learn English.
>   Of course you will be given free time to attend English classes. We live near a very good school of English and have a local theatre. You will have a full day off every week and most evenings free.
>   I am sure you will be very happy with us and you will be treated as one of the family.
>   Looking forward to hearing from you soon.
>
>   Yours sincerely,
>
>   Anne Holdway

Sometimes you will write two or three times to the host family to make arrangements. We have put all the information into one letter, but you do not have to write in exactly the same way.

Accepting a place at college
In some letters of acceptance you do not need to give any more details about yourself, but you may need to send documents.

Ahmad, a student, wrote to accept the place he was offered at a Business School.

Read his letter:

3rd Alley, Jamshidiyeh St.,
Niavaran,
Tehran.

May 15th 1980

London Business School,
103–105 Regent Street,
London WI.

Dear Mr. Taylor,

Thankyou for your letter and the offer of a place on the 1st year Business Studies course. I have great pleasure in accepting the offer. I am enclosing a registration fee of £40.

I look forward to hearing from you again soon with further details.

Yours sincerely,

ABoroumand

A. BOROUMAND

Practice 34 Write a letter accepting each of these offers. You need not write an address.

1. *Dear X,*

   Thank you for your application.

   I am pleased to tell you that we are to offer you a provisional place at the University.

   Please reply as soon as possible if you wish to accept our offer. You should send confirmation of your degree results as soon as they are available.

   I look forward to hearing from you.

   Yours sincerely,
   Y

Note In more formal letters where you are writing the address you are sending your letter to on the left-hand side of the paper, you may also add the name of the person you are writing to, if you know it.

2. *Dear X,*
   Thank you for your letter.

   Unfortunately we are unable to offer you a place on the Economics course as your qualifications are not suitable. However, we suggest you enrol for our 1st year Foundation course in Business Studies and Overseas Marketing.

   We have provisionally reserved a place for you on this course and we would be glad if you would reply as soon as possible if you decide to accept this offer. You should enclose a registration fee of £10 on acceptance.

   We look forward to hearing from you.

   Yours sincerely,
   Y

Refusing an offer
Sometimes, you may not wish to accept the offer in a letter.

How can you refuse politely?
Write a short letter in simple English.

This is one very strange letter Helga received . . .

Dear Helga,

  Your name has been given to me by the WHITE SLAVE AGENCY INC. I have had many au pairs from this agency. My last Italian girl was with me for 8 weeks before she fell ill. I think she lost weight a little too quickly, so I hope you will like our food.

  We live in a room near the railway station which you will share with our 5 children: Daphne 5 months, Chloe 15 months, Rupert 2 years, Charles 3 years and Damian 6 We have a large and friendly dog who seems to love all foreigners.

You will be given some pocket money and your hours will be from 6 a.m. – 9 p.m. every day. After that your time is free.

Our heating is being repaired at the moment, so bring lots of warm woolly clothes.

Looking forward to meeting you.

Yours

Paula Lees

Helga decided to refuse this job. This is what she wrote.

Dear Mrs Smart,

Thank you for your letter offering me an au pair position with your family. I am afraid that I am unable to accept your offer as I have already found a suitable position.

Yours sincerely,

Helga Spohn

If you wish to refuse, first say what you are refusing and then give a general explanation.

This student did not want to accept the offer he had.

Dear X,
Thank you for your offer of a place on the Physics degree course.

I am afraid that I am unable to accept the offer as I have already made other arrangements.

Yours sincerely,
Y

Practice 35 Write a short letter refusing:
1 an offer of accommodation with a shared bedroom
2 an offer of a job in a small village with no facilities to study English

P.S.

Saying yes or no in a letter.

1 Accept politely and confirm what you are accepting . . . or, refuse politely and remind them what you are refusing.
2 Give any information (money, documents, references) that you may have been asked for or that you think is necessary, or give a general reason why you are refusing. Don't write a long letter.
3 End politely. . . .

Don't do this:

Dear X

I don't want your job because I have got a better one.

Best wishes, Y

7 Booking and Buying through the Post

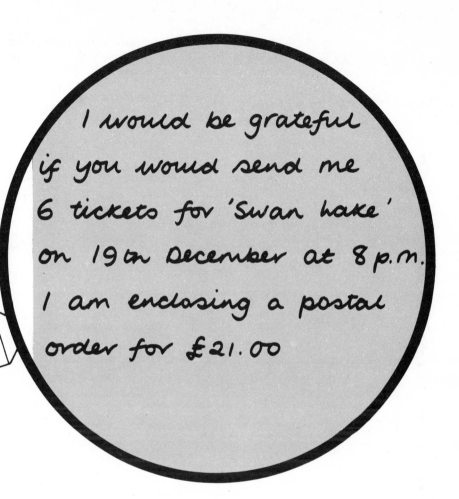

I would be grateful if you would send me 6 tickets for 'Swan Lake' on 19th December at 8 p.m. I am enclosing a postal order for £21.00

You may want to write a letter to buy something you have seen advertised, or something you cannot buy personally. Or you may wish to order, reserve, or book something.

If you live in England you can often do these things by telephone, but when you have to send money you will need to write a letter.

Students studying in Britain often go to the theatre or ballet. Helga, a German girl studying English part-time, decided to go and see 'Swan Lake', a ballet, at Covent Garden in London, with some of her friends.

She wanted six tickets. Each ticket cost £3.50. Read the letter Helga wrote.

15 Homepark Road,
Ealing,
London, W.5

13/12/79

Dear Sir,

I would be grateful if you would send me 6 tickets for 'Swan Lake' on 19th Dec. at 8pm.

I am enclosing a postal order for £21.00 and an s.a.e.

Yours faithfully

Helga Spohn
H. Spohn

You must say

1 politely, what you want *'I would be grateful if . . .'* or *'I would like to . . .'*
2 what you want *'. . . tickets . . .'*
3 how many you want *'six . . .'*
4 if necessary, when you want it for *'. . . 19th December at 8pm . . .'*
5 finally, how much money you are sending *'. . . I am enclosing a *postal order for £21 00*, and if you are writing in Britain, *'. . . a sae . . .'*

You do not need to give personal details about yourself unless it is necessary to do so to buy the correct thing.

Note   postal order = a type of money order used in Britain. If you do not have a bank account in Britain and you cannot write a cheque, then you can send money by a postal order. You can write this in the short form, p.o.

   sae = stamped addressed envelope.
If you want someone to send you something in their reply to your letter, you should enclose an envelope addressed to yourself, and with a stamp on it.

Practice 36 Write a letter for each question. Don't write an address.

1 You want to buy two bags. Beautiful patchwork satin shoulder bags 7" × 8". £4. Send cheque and choice of bright or pastel colours to Magpie, 68 Disraeli Rd. S.W.15.

2 Thousands of secondhand records, all types. Send 15p for list. Stop, Look & Listen, Hayle, Cornwall. (Overseas customers send 3 International Reply Coupons)

If you want to book a holiday you will usually do this on a special form inside a brochure. You can write a letter to ask for a brochure or leaflet, or you can ring up (= make your request by telephone).

You may want to arrange accommodation before you come to Britain, or when you are in the country.
Follow the same rules as for buying things by post in your letter.

You may need to give particular details about yourself or your situation if you want to book something. This helps the person who receives your letter to book the right thing for you. Write this extra information first.

This is a letter Ahmad, a student from Iran, wrote to a hotel in London.

3rd Alley Jamshidiyeh St.,
Niavaran,
Tehran.

July 15th 1980

Dear Sir,
    I would like to book one single room at your hotel for the night of Tuesday, August 1st, 1980

Yours faithfully,

A. Brommond

Ahmad didn't need to give any extra details in that letter, but read this one. It's a little different.

> 3rd Alley Jamshidiyeh St.,
> Niavaran,
> Tehran.
>
> July 15th. 1980
>
> Dear Sir,
> I have been accepted as a student at the London Business School and I am writing to ask you if it is possible to reserve a single room in your hostel from September 2nd – December 10th 1980.
> I look forward to hearing from you.
>
> Yours sincerely
> A.Boroumand
> A. BOROUMAND

Now go on and do the practice.

Practice 37 You write each of these letters. Don't write your own address; just practise the letter. You will need to give a few extra details in some of them.

1 Write to the British Council in your own country to ask if it is possible for them to arrange overnight accommodation for you in London before you travel on to your host family. You are going to work in England as an au pair. You will travel on flight MAS 263, arriving at the air terminal in central London on Tuesday, August 10th, 1982 at 19.00hrs.

2 Write to the Warden of a student hostel, Panda House, 5 Thurloes Rd., London, SW18 7RZ, to apply for a single room for 10 months from October 1980. You have been accepted as a full-time student.

3 Write to order a red, medium size T-shirt. It costs £2.50.

4 Write to buy a copy of a booklet, 'London for Visitors'. It costs 50p and you need to send a sae.

5 Write to book a place on an Intensive English Language course for Technical Students which begins on May 4th. It costs £100, deposit £10. Applicants for this course are asked to state if they require accommodation and if they are willing to share.

P.S.

Letters you write to book or buy something must contain all the necessary information.

Don't write too much . . .

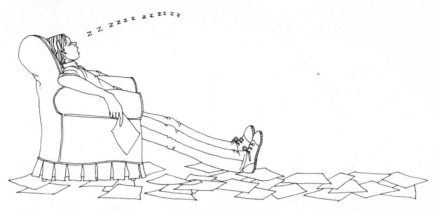

or too little . . .

Write exactly:
1 what you want and, if necessary, the reason why you want to buy or book a particular thing
2 if necessary how many you want
3 if necessary when you want it for
4 if necessary how much money you are sending
5 any other details you need to give or ask for any other information

And remember, separate ideas need separate paragraphs.

8 Problems

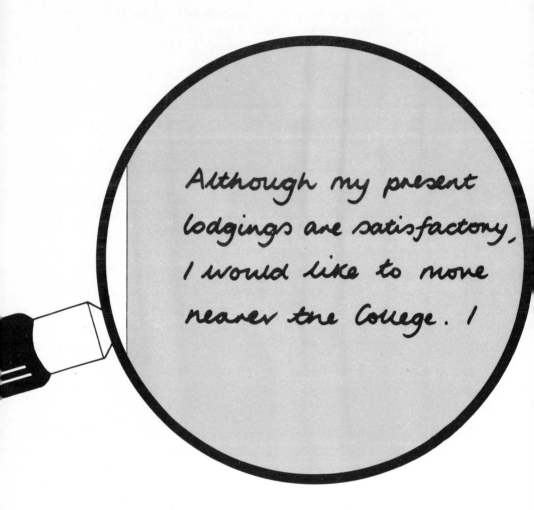

Although my present lodgings are satisfactory, I would like to move nearer the College. I

You can cope with many problems by using the telephone (if you are living in Britain). But sometimes you need to write a letter to explain something, to apologize, or to clear up (solve) some difficulties.

If you have come to live in Britain you may need to renew or extend your visa, or 'permission to stay'. These are formal letters, so write the address of the person or place you are sending your letter to on the left-hand side, a little lower down from your own address. Don't slope this address.

Read this letter from a student who changed his course of study. He had been given permission to stay for nine months. He wants to ask for an extension of his permit.

Room 35, 3 Grange Sq.,
London, WIA 3AA

5/5/81

Home Office,
Lunar House,
Wellesley Road,
Croydon, CR9 2BY

Dear Sir,
   I came to England on September 2nd, 1980 with permission to stay for 9 months.
   I have now changed my course of study and I would like to stay for another year.

Yours faithfully,
A. Boroumand
A. BOROUMAND

This is what Ahmad did:
1 gave a simple explanation of his problem
2 gave a reason
3 said what his plans were

Begin a new paragraph each time.

Changing families
Many girls who work as an au pair in Britain find they are not happy with the family they are living with.
Helga, a German girl, wanted to change the family she was working for. She had a few problems and she also wanted to work in another part of Britain. She talked about the problems with her hostess first, but things didn't get better.
She wrote to the agency that brought her to England.

Practice 38   Read the example and answer the questions. Give short answers.

> 15 Homepark Rd.,
> Ealing,
> London, W.5
> March 6ᵗʰ 1980
>
> Dear Mrs Cade,
>   I am writing to ask you if it is possible for me to work with a different family in another part of England.
>   Although my present family is kind, I am expected to do too much work and do not have enough time to travel round England.
>   I would be grateful if you could manage to place me with another family, preferably in the south of England, not London. I will be free to move at the end of the month.
>
>   Yours sincerely,
>   Helga Spohn (Miss)

1   Why is Helga writing to the agency?
2   What is the most important reason why she wants to leave?
3   Where does she want to move to?
4   Which month will she be free?

Practice 39   Although my present family is kind, I am expected to do too much work.

You try and write a sentence like that about these things.
1   family kind/not enough food
2   plenty of food/unfriendly family
3   lots of free time/have to share a room
4   nice family/not used to looking after very young baby
5   pleasant surroundings/mixed-language family (German wife/British husband)

Problems

Here is a way of asking for something you would like (something you hope is possible) from an employer and the authorities.

I would be grateful if you could . . .

Practice 40   You write a sentence like that about these things
1   forward your suitcase from the airport
2   re-address your letters to your current address
3   change a sweater for one of a larger size
4   send you a free sample of perfume
5   give you Tony's new address

Practice 41   Michelle Munich works as an au pair with a family in the North of England, in a very beautiful but isolated (lonely) village. She wants to practise her English more and there isn't a school nearby. She wants to move to a family in a large town near her friend Helga, who works for the same agency.

You write the letter Michelle would write to the agency which employed her. The address of the agency is on page 41. Michelle lives at 'Lane End', Casterton, Carnforth, Lancs.

Changing course of study
Students sometimes wish to change the course they are studying because the course is unsuitable for them or because they are unsuitable for the course! As usual, it is always best to discuss these problems by speaking to someone first. You may then have to write a letter.

Ahmad, a student, found the first term of his course too easy for him. He had already studied the books at the university in Tehran. He spoke to his tutor, Mr Roxbee, and discussed the matter with him.
He agreed with Ahmad and advised him to write to the Head of the Department.

This is what he wrote:

> Room 35, 3 Grange Sq.,
> London, WIA 3AA
>
> 20/3/81
>
> Dear Professor Pearce,
>   I am a student in the 1st year Business Studies course. I have spoken to my tutor, Mr Roxbee, about moving to the 2nd year of the course because I have already studied

> *most of the 1st year course at University in Tehran.*
> *He agreed with my request and suggested I wrote to you to*
> *make an appointment to discuss the matter.*
>
> *Yours sincerely,*
>
> *Ahmad Boroumand*

Practice 42   These are some students who want to change the course they are studying. Use the information in each question and write a letter like Ahmad's. Just write the letter and not an address.

Remember:

a   say who you are and what you are already studying
b   say who you have talked to about your problem
c   give the reason why you want to change
d   ask for an appointment to discuss or confirm the change

Write to	You are a	You have spoken to	Reason you want to change
1 Dr. Craig	student in Pre-Proficiency course	your teacher	course is too easy, you want to move to Proficiency
2 Mr Tibbetts	student in Accountancy	your tutor, Mr Hamer	you have decided to study Economics instead
3 Miss Carter	student in EFL, Tues. a.m. classes	your class teacher	time is not suitable, you want to study in the evenings

Complaints

You may find problems with things you have bought. If you live in Britain you will probably be able to make your complaint personally, but if you have bought or received something by post, you may need to write a letter about your complaint.

Here is a letter about incorrect details on a driving licence. (You complete a form to apply for a licence.)

---

20 Baleshill Road,
Dorking,
Surrey

DVLC
Swansea,
SA99 1AR
21/7/83

Dear Sir,

I have received my driving licence but some of the details are incorrect.

I would be grateful if you would make the following corrections.

1. My address is 20 Baleshill Road and not 20 Bales Hill Road.

2. My name is Christina Bergos not Christine Bergos.

I look forward to receiving a corrected licence.

Yours faithfully,

(Miss) C. Bergos.

Say:
1 what you are writing about
2 what you hope will be done

Note Christina writes the corrections she wants made to her driving licence as a list. This makes it very clear for the person who will receive your letter to understand.

   I would be grateful if you would . . .

This time you are asking for something to be made better. You expect them to do something about the problem.

Practice 43   If you had a complaint about these things, write the sentence saying what you think should be done to put matters right. The words in brackets give you a suggestion.

Do not write a complete letter.
1 Scratched record (replace).
2 There are incorrect details on your driving licence (make the following corrections).
3 Several pages of a book have been printed twice (refund money).

4   A set of records you have on free trial, but you do not wish to buy them. You want the company to collect them (arrange to collect them).
5   Cancel holiday booking (return deposit).

Helga sent for a T-shirt, but the T-shirt had not arrived after six weeks.

She wrote again:

15, Homepark Road,
Ealing,
London W5
April 10th 1980

Dear Sir,

    I wrote to you on March 6th to order 1 red T-shirt, medium size.

    The T-shirt has still not arrived, and I would be grateful if you would let me know if you received my order and postal order for £1.50

Yours faithfully
(Miss) Helga Spohn

Remember:
a   say when you wrote the first letter
b   give the reason you wrote before
c   give the reason you are writing again
d   ask if they received your first letter or order (if you sent money) or repeat your request

Here is a letter about some brochures:

Dear Sir,

I wrote to you some time ago for your Scottish Ski brochure, but I have not received any reply.

I would be grateful if you would send me the brochure as soon as possible.

Yours faithfully

(Miss) Tina Pearce

Practice 44 Can you write a letter about each problem?

1 Helga wrote a letter to ask about museums and special exhibitions at Easter in London, but she didn't get an answer to her letter.

2 Ahmad sent for a copy of the leaflet 'London for Visitors', and he enclosed a postal order for 50p. He waited three weeks but the leaflet did not come.

3 Ahmad sent for some free brochures that were offered in an advertisement about a new sports car. He didn't get an answer to his letter.

4 Helga complained about a ballet she went to because the performance had been changed at the last minute, and she wanted a refund or some more tickets for the ballet that was advertised. She did not get a reply to her letter of complaint.

It's a good idea to keep a copy of any letter you send in which you have asked for or ordered something, or in which you have given information you may need to know about later. Your letter does not have to be typed. You can copy your letter with a photocopying machine in a shop or a library, or at a large railway station.

If you live in Britain you may receive official letters from a Government Department, or the authorities. Some need a reply, others do not. Sometimes you can reply by telephone.

Practice 45   Read each of the following letters and decide whether you need to write a letter in reply or not. If you decide you do not need to write, say in one sentence what you would do.

Dear Sir or Madam

Our records show the following books have been issued in your name and are now 4 weeks overdue.

Please return the books as soon as possible.

Yours faithfully,

G.P. Thomas
Chief Librarian

Murder on the Orient Express: A. Christie
Jaws: Peter Benchley

Glynns
Bank
Limited

160 Brompton Road,
London, SW7 3JG
Telephone (01) 405 7534

Our ref   MC/JEE

October 5th, 1980

Mr. A. Boroumand,
Room 35,
Overseas Student Hostel,
3, Grange Square,
London, W1A 3AA.

Dear Mr. Boroumand,

With reference to your application to open an account with the Bank, would you be good enough to call at this Branch at 9 a.m. on Thursday, October 16th, in order to sign the necessary documents.

Please confirm that this time is convenient.

Yours truly,

M. Craft
M CRAFT
ASSISTANT MANAGER

Note   truly is sometimes used instead of faithfully

```
                    Home
                    Office
                 Lunar House Wellesley Road Croydon CR9 2BY
                    Telephone (Immigration) 01-686 0688
                         (Nationality)  01-681 3421
                    Telegram IMMNAT CROYDON
                              Please reply to
                              The Under Secretary of State
                              Your reference
                              Our reference  F 107183
                              Date  10 June, 1981

    Dear Mr. Boroumand,

    Thank you for your letter.

    I am writing to say that extension of your student residence visa
    is conditional on evidence of full-time study in the U.K., and
    evidence of means.

    Please forward the appropriate documents to this office, together
    with your passport.

    Yours sincerely,

    A. Bateson
```

You need only write a letter in reply to 3.

Practice 46 Look at the letter from the Home Office again.
Many official letters have references and/or instructions.
1   What is the reference on this letter?
2   Who must Ahmad reply to?
3   Write the address he should send his letter to
4   What must he send with the letter?
    a
    b
    c

Note   evidence = anything that gives a reason for believing
something. Here it would mean a letter from your College to say
you were a full-time student.

means = resources, the way in which you are going to support
yourself, i.e. if you have enough money to live on.

Write any reference underneath the address you are sending your·
letter to. This helps the authorities to answer your letter quickly.

Here is the letter Ahmad wrote in reply. He typed his letter this time. He writes a list in the same way as Christina did in her letter about her driving licence.

```
                                          Room 35, Overseas Student Hostel,
                                          3, Grange Sq.,
The Under Secretary of State,             London, W1A 3AA
Home Office,
Lunar House, Wellesley Road,              15th June 1981
Croydon, CR9 2BY

Dear Sir,

Thank you for your letter, ref. F107183

My new course of study begins in September 1981 and will end in September
1982.

1)  I enclose a letter from the College

2)  photocopies of my Bank statements

3)  my passport, no. 2435

Yours faithfully,

A. Boroumand
```

Apologies

If things go wrong and it's your fault, you will need to make an apology. Again, if you live in Britain you may be able to do this by telephone, but it is always polite to write a letter as well.

If you are studying full-time in Britain and you do not attend several classes, you might receive a letter like this:

Dear Mr. Boroumand,
I notice that you have been absent from tutorials and lectures for nearly a week. I would be glad if you would come and see me about this.
Yours,
George Roxbee

Practice 47 Answer these questions.
1 Why is Mr Roxbee writing to Ahmad?
2 What should Ahmad do?

There are many occasions when you need to write a letter; if you cannot telephone, or if you live a long way away, or if you want to make sure your explanation is recorded in writing.

Here is a letter someone wrote because they missed an appointment

> *Dear Mr X,*
> *I am writing to apologize for missing my appointment yesterday afternoon. I am afraid I was not well and I was unable to *'phone to cancel the appointment.*
>
> *If it is possible I would like to make another appointment for the same time next week.*
>
> *Yours sincerely,*
> *Y*

Note 'phone = short form of 'telephone'

Here is how to write a letter of apology.
1 apologize. *'I am writing to apologize for . . .'*
2 say what you did wrong *'missing my appointment . . .'*
3 give a reason (tell the truth if possible!) *'. . . I am afraid I was not well . . .'*
4 say what you will do to put matters right *'. . . Is it possible to . . .' 'I hope it is possible to . . .' '. . . I would like to . . .' 'I would be grateful if . . .' '. . . I hope I can . . .'*

Practice 48 Here are some things that have happened to you. The remedy is the method of putting something right.
Can you write three letters making an apology about each problem you have had? Choose a suitable reason and remedy to write in each letter.

PROBLEM	REASON	REMEDY
your bank account is overdrawn	you made a mistake with the dates	you want to make another appointment
you missed a dental appointment	the monthly money from your parents is late	you will soon have additional funds credited to your account
you failed to attend an oral exam	you overslept	you hope it is possible to retake the exam at a later date

Don't write the greeting or the ending and signature in these letters, but remember you will usually know the name of the person you are writing to apologize to, so the ending will be 'Yours sincerely,'.

P.S.

Don't do this!

> Dear Sir,
>
> Can you lend me some money this month because I have none.
>
> Regards,
>
> Mick

. . . the bank will not be pleased.

Any letters about problems must state clearly what the problem is and your suggestion about putting matters right.

9 Letters to Friends

I went to the cinema three times last week to see 'Star Wars'. I think you would enjoy this film. You must see it when you can.

Do write soon, please give my love to your Mother,

love

If you are studying or working in Britain, you will meet many other foreigners as well as, (we hope), some English people . . .

As you won't speak every foreign language, you will probably use English to speak to and write to your friends.

Reasons for writing

If you are like everybody else, you probably don't write to your friends as often as you should!

You can begin your letter by making a little apology like this:
Example:

> *I'm sorry I haven't written for such a long time/so long*
> *but . . .* (give a reason)

Practice 49   Write an apology and add these reasons each time.
1   you've been ill
2   you've been studying for exams
3   you've been very busy

Or you can begin your letter by asking how your friend is, like this:
Example:

> *How are you?*

Usually these two openings, apologizing for not writing before and asking how your friend is, go together. It doesn't matter which order you choose.

> *Dear X,*
> *How are you? I'm sorry I haven't written for such a long time*
> *but I've been very busy.*

> *Dear X,*
> *I'm sorry I haven't written for such a long time but I've been*
> *very busy. How are you?*

Don't go on writing question after question in your letter: it won't be very interesting.

Topics

Next you should go on to say what you have been doing since you last saw, or wrote to, your friend. This means your friend will know your news. If you only ask questions they won't know what you have been doing. Begin a new paragraph because this is something new.

Note   You cannot write *'I've been busy'* because it does not sound very polite; always add *'very'*.

Practice 50   Describe what you have been doing for the last month. Tell the truth! Write 2 sentences.

Remember these things about using the past tense

1   If what you did is finished, use the *past* tense.
Example:

> *I took the first year course in Business Studies but it was too*
> *easy.*

2   If you started something and you are still doing it, use the
present perfect continuous tense.
Example:

> *I have been studying the second year course since September.*

3   With some adverbs, 'last week', 'yesterday', you need to use the
simple past. The action you are talking about may be continuous
but you do not need to show that it happened between two
points in time.
Example:

> *This morning we cooked some food for a picnic.*

Practice 51   Here are some things you have been doing. Write them as
sentences and join the sentences together. Check that the way you
join the sentences together makes sense.

1   reading a lot of difficult books for your course —— gambling too
much at night
2   looking after the children during the day —— going out at night
to a good new club with your friends
3   went to a film yesterday —— planning a tour of England during
the summer
4   enrolled in a pottery class —— met an interesting Greek boy in
the class
5   working hard —— going to a lot of parties because it's
Christmas
6   feeling ill —— staying at home and watching a lot of television
7   losing weight —— eating healthy food to keep fit
8   going out with a new boy/girlfriend —— spending a lot of
money

In letters to your friends you do not need to begin a new paragraph
for every new idea. Sometimes one idea continues from another.

You can continue your letter by talking about something in more
detail. Read the opening paragraphs of this letter.

> *Dear Y,*
> *I'm sorry I haven't written for so long but I've been studying for*
> *my exams. How are you?*
>
> *I've been reading a lot of new books for my course and gambling*
> *too much at night! I went to the 'Fleece Me' club in Golden*
> *Square last week with some friends from college. They won, but*
> *I lost nearly £200!*

Practice 52   Look back at *Practice 51* Choose four things and write in more detail
about them. Write one or two more sentences each time.

Feelings
This is the place in your letter to describe how you feel about the things you talk about.
Ahmad lost money gambling.
He felt:
fed-up
annoyed
cross
angry

Helga met a boy she liked at a student's party, but he got very drunk and didn't treat her properly.
She felt:
upset
embarrassed
awkward

At the same party Michelle, Helga's friend, met an older man who was a teacher at the college. She enjoyed his company.
She felt:
interested
happy
fascinated

Practice 53 What would your feeling be if you:
1. failed an exam
2. lost some money
3. met a new boyfriend
4. bought a set of records you had wanted for a long time
5. booked a holiday
6. went to a *pub and had a good evening with your friends
7. broke your landlady's chair
8. had a quarrel with a good friend
9. ate some different foreign food for the first time
10. went to a dinner party where you had to speak English all the time

Note *pub = public house. A place where you can drink, (if you are over eighteen), sometimes eat, and meet your friends

Practice 54 Read the opening paragraphs of this letter and tick √ the sentences that have been written about:
apologizing for not writing
greeting a friend
describing something
feelings

> *Dear Joseph,*
> *Sorry I haven't written for a long time but I have been very busy. How are you?*
>
> *Last month I moved house because I had a quarrel with my landlady. I was very upset because she wouldn't give me a key*

to the house. It was very embarrassing to ring on the door every time I came home, especially when I wanted to be late.

Practice 55   You try and write these letters. Don't write an address and don't sign the letter. This is practice about what to write in the letter. Begin Dear X each time.

1   You have been to a party. You met someone you liked and you are talking about this to your friend.
2   You have a new teacher for your class. You are talking about him or her to your friend.
3   You have been away for the weekend with the family you work for as an au pair. You are talking to your friend about this.
4   You saw this in the street:

Write and talk about it to your friend.
5   Write a letter describing what you have done in the last month. If possible post this letter to someone.

Look at Chapter 4 pages 28–33 to check you have written the envelope correctly.

Writing to someone you know and have seen recently.
In these letters to your friends you can 'gossip' (talk about other people's affairs). You don't need to write so much about what you have been doing, because they know.
In these letters you usually have too many things to talk about, so remember these guides.
Choose tenses carefully. Don't translate your ideas.

Practice 56   Read this.

Most countries have public holidays. The word holiday comes from 'holy' day, when people were expected to go to church and pray. Since the Reformation however, holidays, or 'holy' days, have been celebrated as an excuse to relax and enjoy oneself after a hard day's work.

England has probably the fewest holidays in Europe. It is only recently that New Year's Day was made a holiday, and that was because so few people came to work that day that the government gave up saying they should work.

You couldn't really use anything like that in a letter. It's not written as a letter but as an essay, so it's no use just adding *'Dear X,'* at the beginning and *'Yours sincerely,'* at the end.

Letters to friends are like talking to them. This doesn't mean you write exactly as you speak, but letters to friends are not formal: they are friendly and private.
In your friendly letters:
1   show your personality (the way you think and feel about things)
2   give the atmosphere (what something was like, where, and when it happened)
3   above all, be friendly

Practice 57   Now read this and compare it with the essay in *Practice 56*.

> *Dear X,*
> *I've just got back from a trip to the sea-side with my family. We went on Friday and came back today (Tuesday), because Mr Y had an extra day off.*
>
> *I still don't understand these English. Why do they call a holiday a 'bank' holiday? Anyway, we had a good time. The baby fell in the water twice, and the other children ate too much ice-cream and were sick, but thank God, for once it was hot so I am BROWN at last. Holidays are harder work than the rest of the time!*
>
> *Write soon,*
> *love,*
> *Y*

Practice 58   Read what is written and pick out what you would put in a letter. You can tick √ each point you think you should include.

Most English people are very suspicious of foreigners. It isn't a myth that they are insular, and it would be surprising if they weren't since England is part of the British Isles.

Insularity is, or can be, rather dangerous. It breeds a form of superiority which can often turn into ignorant political judgement.

The British, and in particular the English, have never really accepted the fact that they have at last joined Europe. Calais still marks the point of no return.

Did you get these points?
1   English people are suspicious of foreigners
2   because they live on an island
3   there is a great deal of snobbery
4   the English don't like the Common Market

Read this letter.

Dear X,

I'm SO angry, and it's not the first time. Just when you think you understand these bloody people, you realise you don't. It's a cold island and it makes cold people. My tutor took us out for a drink yesterday: he was really nice and friendly. Today, he doesn't know us; he's just coldly polite.

They didn't join the Common Market; Europe joined them. I'll never understand what makes them tick as long as I live. How about the Scots? How do you find them?
Love,
   Y

Practice 59   Now try and write your own short letter to a friend about English people. You should try and include some experience you have had.

Practice 60   Here are some subjects you know something about personally. Choose any *two* and write a letter to a friend you know. Concentrate on making your sentences short and correct.
1   older people
2   boy/girlfriends
3   problems, personal or financial
4   loneliness

P.S.

You won't have many friends if you write this sort of letter . . .

> *Dear Colin,*
> *How are you? Did you get my letter? Are you studying hard?*
> *Do you remember the fun we had on our summer holiday?*
>
> *Well I must go now. Please excuse my bad English.*
> *Bye-bye,*
> > *Derek*

because you might get this reply . . .

> *Dear Derek,*
> *I am well. Yes. Yes. Yes.*
> *Yours,*
> *Colin*

1   Starting the letter:
> apologise for not writing before
> say why you are writing
> ask how your friend is

2   Then:
> talk about what you have been doing
> write in more detail about a particular thing
> comment on your feelings about what you are writing about
> make sure you have said all you want to say

3   Finally:
> end your letter in a friendly way
> show that you hope they will write a letter back to you

10 Follow-up

Can I ask you a favour? Could you send me the latest 'Mothercare' catalogue?

You will write letters to your friends when you are living in Britain and when you return home, but there is another kind of letter you may need or want to write:

    you may want some information from the college where you studied;

    you may need to make an arrangement about something;

    you may want someone to forward your letters to you;

    you may want to ask someone to send something to you that you used to buy yourself in Britain.

This type of letter is a little like letters of enquiry, (Chapter 5 pages 34–46) and letters booking or buying something by post, (Chapter 7 pages 57–61), but this time the person you are writing to has already met you, or you know them. These letters are a mixture of friendly and formal letters.

Follow-up

Read this letter from a student:

> 94, Phillipoupoleos st.,
> Athens, GREECE
>
> August 4th 1980
>
> Dear Mrs Ager,
>   I was a student in Proficiency II from Sept. 1979 – July 1980. My teacher was Mr. Jarvis.
>   I have returned home earlier than expected and I would be grateful if you would forward my exam results to the above address.
>   Many thanks,
>   Yours sincerely,
>   Macia Eelonidou

You should:
1 identify yourself
2 explain why you are writing
3 ask for what you want
4 finally say thank you: '*Many thanks*' or '*Thank you for your help*'.

Note Macia did not write the address of the college on the left-hand side. Her letter was half friendly and half formal and you can choose whether to put this address or not.

Practice 61 You write each of these letters. Use your own home address where necessary.
1 Helga wrote to her teacher, Miss Ayton, to ask for a certificate of attendance and a reference because she wanted to attend English classes in Germany. You write the letter to the teacher to ask for these things.
2 You have returned home but you have not got all the addresses of the friends in your English class at college in England. You think the college might have a list of these addresses. Write to the Secretary and ask her if she can help you with the address of Marie Scarpato and Karin Labbi.
3 You have returned home. You forgot to give your landlady, Mrs Pye, your home address. Write to her to tell her the address and ask her to send on to you (forward) any mail.

4   Write to the Warden, Mr Blake, of the student hostel you lived
    in to ask him if he could let you know if the gold pen you lost
    has been found, and if it has, to send it to you at your home
    address.

Here is a letter Ahmad wrote to his Bank Manager because he
forgot to close his bank account:

3rd Alley, Jamshidiyeh St.,
Niavaran,
Tehran, IRAN.

26/8/82

The Manager,
Glynns Bank Ltd.,
160 Brompton Rd.,
London S.W.3.

Dear Mr. Croft,
        I have an account at your bank, no. 00476382,
but I have now returned home and I would be grateful if
you would arrange to close my account and credit any
funds to my account here. The address is:
        Bank Saadi,
        Ave. Ferdowsi,
        Tehran, Iran.
        I am sorry that I was unable to arrange this
personally but I returned home earlier than planned.
Thank you for your help.

                    Yours sincerely,
                    A Boroumand
                    A. BOROUMAND

Practice 62   Can you check that Ahmad has done all these things in his letter?
Mark each point with a tick √.
1   he has identified himself
2   he has explained why he is writing
3   he has asked for what he wants to be done
4   he has thanked the Manager

Helga had been an au pair in England and she liked the clothes the
children in the family wore. She bought some clothes from
Mothercare to give to her friends at home. When she arrived home

many of her friends asked her if she could get some things for them, so Helga wrote to her hostess. This is her letter:

> 154 Horb 1/Rexingen,
> Allemandestrasse 15,
> West Germany.
> 11/12/81
>
> Dear Evelyn,
>   I arrived home safely and I miss England already.
>   I'd like to ask you a favour. Can you send me a pair of the gingham shoes from Mothercare like Harriet's, but size 10.? I'd be very grateful if you could also send me 6 vests and 6 pairs of pants, white, size 80 cms.
>   Please let me know how much they cost and I will send you a money order.
>   Love to the children,
>   Best wishes,
>   Helga

Practice 63 Write a similar letter asking for the following things:
1 ask your hostess to look for a blue silk shirt you think you left behind
2 ask your friend, Peter, if he can send you the latest Led Zeppelin L.P. (long playing) record
3 ask your hostess if she can send on the slides you sent to be developed but which had not arrived before you returned home
4 write and ask your friend, Christos, if he could buy you another set of slides of Oxford and send them to you because your slides were no good
5 ask your friend Liz, if she can arrange to get the Mothercare catalogue to you

Keeping in touch with friends
Letters you write to your friends when you have returned home and you are not likely to see them for some time should tell them something about the changes in your life since your return.

Ahmad wrote this letter to a friend:

3rd Alley, Jamshidiyeh St.,
Niavaran,
Tehran.

16/9/82

Dear Paul,

It seems a long time since I was last in England.
I have been at my parents' home for 2 months now, but I
still think about London and all the friends I met.

I stopped in Greece on my way home and had a
very good time. It's a very interesting country.

There have been a lot of changes here since I left.
Many of my friends have got married and have got
jobs. I suppose I will have to start looking for a job soon too.

Please write soon. Why don't you come and visit
Iran? You are always welcome and we have plenty of room.
Take care,

Ahmad

1 Give some information about your journey back. You can
  describe the journey and make some comments about your
  feelings.
2 Write about what you find when you return home. Things will
  probably have changed.
3 Write about your plans for the future.
4 You can suggest your friend visits you or you arrange a meeting
  for the future.

Note *Take care* = this is another way men especially could end a
letter to a friend.

Practice 64 1 Helga went home by train via France. She stayed with friends in Paris for three days and got ill from eating too much rich food. Her family were pleased to see her but Helga was disappointed to find nothing had changed in her home town. Her sister had a new haircut and a new boyfriend.

After a few weeks Helga started work as a secretary in a Chemical firm. It is well-paid but boring work.

Write the letter Helga wrote to her friend Michelle who was still in England.

It may help you to divide the information in this question into the groups on page 88 before you write the letter.

2 Peter Jenson left England after his Finals. He passed his degree in Accountancy. He arrived home in Switzerland three months ago. He thought it would be easy to get a job, but he was not able to find one. He didn't like living with his parents after his independence in England.

He wrote to his friend Thomas, and asked him about the chances of getting a job in England. He was also rather sad because his girl-friend, Cathy, was English. He hoped that she would visit him soon.

Write the letter he wrote.

Read the example of Ahmad's letter on page 88. It will help you write these letters.

Other arrangements
You may wish to make arrangements to stay with people, or you may have to deliver something for one of your friends. The pattern for your letter is the same as for the other arrangements.

Read this letter:

59, Wellington Road,
Twickenham,
Middlesex.
1st June, 1982.

Dear Mrs. Hopkins,

I am a friend of Jani's in England and I am returning home next month. I wonder if it is convenient if I visit you briefly on Tuesday, 31st August?

I hope it will be possible to meet you, but please don't make any special arrangements.

Yours sincerely,

Pippa Leverton.

Practice 65   Write two short letters. Make sure you have included all the information.

1   You would like to stay for a few nights with some friends of your friend, David, when you go back home through France from Britain. You don't know how to get to their house from the station because you haven't visited France before.

2   You have a parcel to deliver to your parents' friends when you come to study in Britain. You have to arrange how to deliver it to them, and how to find their house because you are a newcomer to Britain.

P.S.

You will not be popular if you write like this . . .

Dear Jani,

I want you to send me 2 dozen Babygros, some jumpers and all the latest pop records.

lots of love,

Pippa

As usual, you should explain:
1 why you are writing
2 what you would like the person to do
3 send any money if you want something sent on to you as postage is expensive!

11 Postcards, Greetings Cards, Notes

The last chapter in this book is about a different way of writing to people: this is by writing on a postcard, or on a greeting card, or in the form of short note.

Postcards
Sometimes you won't want to write a letter to a friend. You can send them a postcard instead. You often send a postcard to your friends when you are on a holiday.

This is not a letter, so don't write it like a letter. There isn't much space, so make it short.

Look at this postcard from Helga to her friend.

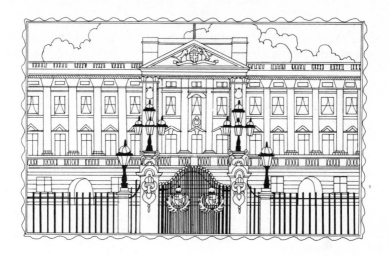

On the back Helga wrote;

The message is short. You don't need to write full sentences. You can often leave out personal pronouns (I/you/he/she/it/we/they), and words that you would use in full sentences (the definite and indefinite articles, 'the' and 'a', and verbs).

Practice 66   Here are some sentences from a letter. You can take a few words away and you can still understand the meaning.

After each group of sentences there is a number in brackets. You try and take this number of words out of the group of sentences. Draw a line through each word that you think you could take away.

Example:

~~The~~ weather ~~is~~ beautiful. ~~We have seen some~~ marvellous cities and I ~~have met some~~ interesting people, especially a Swedish boy ~~called~~ Bjorn! (12)

1   The life hasn't changed in this village. It's very peaceful. I'm returning by bus next week, is it possible for you to meet me at the station? (10)

   Note   I'm = one word; *it's* = one word.

2   We have just arrived here. The weather is very warm. I've still got a dreadful cold. Brian is fine and we both send our love to you. (13)

Read the words that are left. They should still make sense.

Practice 67   Here are some more sentences from a letter. This time you try and make each one short so that they are suitable to write on a postcard. You may leave out some words and put others in a different order if you wish, but don't change the meaning.

Example:

On Sunday we went on a picnic which was very good. I have bought lots of baskets because they are very cheap in the market here.

Went on a good picnic Sunday. Bought lots of cheap baskets in market.

1   I saw Liz last week. She is much fatter than she was when I saw her at Christmas. I think the good food here is the reason why she is so happy and wants to stay for another year.

2   The weather isn't very good but we're going on a boat trip tomorrow. I wish you were here with us, but we'll see you when we get back next week.

Look again at Helga's p.c. (You can shorten 'postcard' like this). She uses some other common abbreviations you can write on p.cs.

& = and

v = very

Note   You can use your initials instead of your full name if the person you are sending the p.c. to will understand who has sent it. (They know you well.)

Look again at Helga's postcard with the picture of Buckingham Palace. (This is where the Queen of England lives). She wrote something about the picture on the postcard.

Practice 68   Look at each postcard and write a comment about each picture.

Practice 69   Add a suitable comment about the weather. Helga wrote that it was 'very cold' on her postcard.

The date

Write the date at the top of the postcard. Always use the short form. (see chapter 1).

The address

In many countries you do not write the address on a postcard and send it through the post. You put the card in an envelope first. You do not do this in Britain. Write the address in the space provided on the postcard. Check about how to write an outside address in Chapter 4. The only thing different about your postcard is that if you want to send it to all the family, or to many people, there is not enough space to write everyone's name. You can also write like this on an envelope if you wish.

Tim, Sue, Daisy and Sam Browne,
20 Coleshill Road,
Teddington,
Middlesex.

The Brownes
or All the Brownes
or The Browne family
or All at 20 Coleshill Road,
Teddington,
Middlesex. –

If you write to a group of friends who all live in the same flat, you could write:

All at,
Flat 3, 121 Benion Rd.,

Summary

You send postcards to friends to greet them, and usually from a holiday. It would be unusual to say anything serious.

Greetings Cards (Christmas, New Year, Birthday, or other special event cards)

You can use a Christmas or birthday card to send a short message to someone. This is called 'keeping in touch'.
You may want to give a friend your new address or tell them you are going to write soon.

You can write a short and simple letter inside a card. Here is a Christmas card Ahmad sent to his friend

1 You do not need to begin 'Dear'.
2 Some people write a full letter and enclose it on a piece of paper inside a card, but if you write on the card it is best to make your greeting short.
3 Write your address (if you want) at the bottom of the card. You would do this if you had moved, or if you had not written to this person for a long time. You do not need to set out address in a sloping line. Just make sure it is clear.

Many people only write to someone at Christmas or the New Year. They write all the interesting things that have happened in the year in a short way.

Read this card:

36 Homepark Rd,
Dulwich
London
SE21

Married Kurt in Jan.,
moved to London in
March, had a baby
girl in October.
We're going to the
States in Feb. Do
get in touch

love
Helen
x

Practice 70 Imagine you are sending a Christmas card to a friend you have not written to for a year. Give your news of the year briefly, in about six short sentences. If you fold a piece of paper to the same size as a card, you will have practice in writing in a smaller space.

Notes and Messages
There is another kind of short letter you may need to write, called a note or message. A letter is not necessary in these situations:
1 you call round to see someone who is not there
2 you need to tell someone about a telephone call for them
3 you leave a message for the milkman or other tradesman
4 you leave a message for your landlady
5 you return something you have borrowed

You can write a message on any kind of paper. (Some people even write on the wall . . . this is not a good idea!) It doesn't matter how you arrange your writing. It is a way of giving information to someone quickly.

Practice 71 Read the following notes which correspond to situations 1–5 described above. They are not in the same order. Decide which note is suitable for which situation.

a TOM

THANKS FOR LOAN OF THE SCARF.
IT KEPT ME V. WARM ON THE WAY HOME
SONIA

b Dear Mrs Pye,
Back at 8pm. Please don't wait for me to eat.
Ahmad

c milkman
No milk today.
2 pints Monday
Thanks

d Pat Tom called. Please phone
soon as poss. 246 8068

e Sue – called round to see if you could come out tonight, but no-one in. See you in class tomorrow. Tim

Note Use '*Dear*' in a note if you are writing to someone who is older than you. It is a sign of respect.

Practice 72 Here are some situations. Try and write each one as a note. Make
sure you have included all the important points.

1   Ahmad called round to his friend's house to return a
gramophone record. No-one answered the door. Ahmad didn't
think it was safe to leave the record outside the flat. He asked
his friend to 'phone him as soon as he got back so he could
bring the record round. He suggested they should go out and eat
together. Write the note he left for his friend.

2   You thought you would be home for supper with your landlady
but some friends called unexpectedly and took you out to eat.
You won't be home until late and you haven't got a key. Write a
note to your landlady, Mrs Fiddick, about this.

3   You return a book to a friend. You leave it in his room because
he's not there. Thank him for the book which you enjoyed
because it made you think a lot. Write the note to put in the
book when you return it.

4   Your hostess has left you alone for the weekend. She is
returning on Monday with some guests. She wants three more
pints of milk and some single cream. Write a note to leave in the
milkbottle for the milkman.

5   Take this telephone message and leave it for your friend.

Thank-you Notes

Although it is not very common in Britain now to write a letter to thank someone for a meal, it is a polite thing to do. Of course, you must always write to thank people if you have been given something. The pattern to follow is the same whether you are writing a short note, or as part of a friendly letter.

You often write this kind of note on a greetings card or on a pretty card.

1   Say thank-you for what you received.
2   Make a short comment about what you are saying thank you for.
3   Choose a suitable way of ending and signing your name (see Chapter 3).

Read this thank-you note

Dear Mrs Fiddick,

Thank you very much for inviting me to meet the family. I enjoyed myself very much indeed and the food was delicious.

Yours sincerely,
Rebecca

Practice 73   Write these thank-you notes:

1   You received a book as a present from a friend of your host family. Her name is Melanie Gibbs and she is married.
2   Your tutor took all your English class to a celebration meal at the end of term. His name is Mr Isaacs.

Note   You should always write a letter to say thank you to your hostess or landlady you lived with if you were studying or working in Britain. This will be part of a friendly letter (see Chapter 10).

Practice 1　You can put any number before any street name.
96 Cambridge Street,　　53 Rosemont Road,
20 Twyford Avenue,　　12 Lunesdale Drive,
143 Homepark Road,

Practice 2　Example answers:
Top flat,　　　　　　　Flat 2B,
　96 Cambridge Street,　　53 Rosemont Road,
Flat 2,
　143 Homepark Road,

Practice 3　Example answers:
96 Cambridge St.,　　　53 Rosemont Rd.,
　Ware,　　　　　　　　Marlow,
20 Twyford Ave.,　　　12 Lunesdale Drive,
　Saltash,　　　　　　　Carnforth,
143 Homepark Rd.,
　Aberdeen,

Practice 4　96 Cambridge St.,　　　53 Rosemont Rd.,
　Ware,　　　　　　　　Marlow,
　　Herts.　　　　　　　　Bucks.
20 Twyford Ave.,　　　12 Lunesdale Drive,
　Saltash,　　　　　　　Carnforth,
　　Cornwall.　　　　　　　Lancs.
143 Homepark Rd.,
　Aberdeen,
　　Scotland.

Practice 6　Marlborough House,　　101 Park Road,
　Homepark Road,　　　Winterton,
　Saltash,　　　　　　　Lincs.
　　Cornwall.　　　　168 Rosendale Ave.,
15 Haverfield Gdns.,　　Dulwich,
　Kew,　　　　　　　　London,
　　Surrey,　　　　　　　SE21 8SZ
　　　TW9 1JA　　　39 Alfred Road,
Flat 1,　　　　　　　Farnham,
　391 Clapham Road,　　Surrey.
　London,
　　SW4 7UT

Practice 7　1　×　　4　×
　　　　　　2　√　　5　×
　　　　　　3　×　　6　√

Practice 8 Example answers:
  a 22nd April, 1983   **b** 3/6/82
     March 23rd, 1985   7.8.87
     4th April, 1981   31/5/79

Practice 10 1 Dear Sir, (or Madam)
  2 Dear Sir, (or Madam)
  3 Dear Isabella,
  4 Dearest Sebastian, or Dearest Marion,
  5 Dear Mrs Pye,
  6 Dear Mr Pye,
  7 Dear Mr Fiddick,
  8 Dear Annie,

Practice 11

15 Haverfield Gdns.,
Richmond,
Surrey.
31/8/79

Dear Sir,

Practice 12 with example signatures:
  1 Yours faithfully,   5 Yours sincerely,
       (Mrs) C. Jarvis   Carol Jarvis
  2 Yours faithfully,   6 Yours sincerely,
       (Mrs) C. Jarvis   Carol Jarvis
  3 Love,   7 Yours sincerely,
       Carol   Carol Jarvis
  4 Lots of love,   8 Best wishes, (or Love,)
       Carrie   Carol

Practice 13 Yours faithfully,
       (your name in full)

Practice 14 1 ×
  2 √
  3 √

Practice 15 You can write the address sloped or straight.
  1 Visa Dept.,
       Home Office,
         Lunar House,
           Wellesley Rd.,
             CROYDON,
               CR9 2BY
  2 Miss J. Fisher, (or Miss Jane Fisher, or Jane Fisher,)
       121 Addison Way,
         LONDON, N.W.11.

3 Subscription Dept.,
   BBC Modern English,
    Modern English Publications,
    33 Shaftesbury Avenue,
    LONDON, W1V 7DD

4 Neuler Pecenha,
   24 Thornton Road,
   Acton,
   LONDON, W.3.

5 Dr Charles Carter,
   The Principal,
    Abbey Language School,
    12 Abbey Road,
    HIGH WYCOMBE
    Bucks,
    ENGLAND

Practice 16 1 Dear Sir,
I would be grateful if you would tell me where I can buy a copy of the handbook 'How to Apply for Admission to a University'.

Yours faithfully,
(sign your name)

2 Dear Sir,
I would be grateful if you would send me a list of schools in London where I can take a short course in English language during the summer.

Yours faithfully,
(sign your name)

3 Dear Sir,
I would be grateful if you would send me a timetable for trains to Scotland from King's Cross.

Yours faithfully,
(sign your name)

4 Dear Sir,
I would be grateful if you would send me details and information about how I can apply to study at an English school.

Yours faithfully,
(sign your name)

5 Dear Sir,
I would be grateful if you would send me any information about special exhibitions and events in Oxford over Easter.

Yours faithfully,
(sign your name)

6 Dear Sir,
I would be grateful if you would send me an application form for membership of the Ealing Squash Club.

Yours faithfully,
(sign your name)

7 Dear Sir,
I would be grateful if you would send me the latest Mothercare catalogue.

Yours faithfully,
(sign your name)

8 Dear Sir,
I would be grateful if you would give me details of the rates for a double room with all meals at your hotel.

Yours faithfully,
(sign your name)

Practice 20

	your ability	your interests	your plans	your age	your sex	your nationality
1			✓	✓		✓
2		✓	✓	✓	✓	
3		✓	✓	✓	✓	✓
4			✓			✓

Practice 21 Example answer for question 1.
Dear Sir,
I would be grateful if you would send me details of how I can work as an au pair in England.

I am a 25 year-old Japanese girl and I would like to come to England next year for one year.

Yours faithfully,
(sign your name)

Practice 22 **1a** finding au pair work
        1b I would be grateful if you would send me details about working as an au pair
        2a September
        2b I would like to take an English course in the summer
        3a she wanted to know what kind of school it was and how big it was
        3b Would you please send me details about your school
        4   enrolment form and deposit
        5   I am enclosing an International Reply Coupon

Practice 24
   1a Business Study courses
   1b I would be grateful if you would send me information about Business Study courses at your school
   3a he asked for advice about his qualifications
   3b I would be grateful for your advice about a suitable course to study
   4a certificates
   4b references
   4c reply coupon

Practice 26 Example answer for question 3.   your own address
The Registrar,
St. Godric's Secretarial College,
14 Fitzroy Ave.,
West Hampstead,
London N.3.

Dear Sir,
I would be grateful if you would send me information about secretarial courses at your college.

I am an 18 year-old Lebanese girl. I have not studied shorthand or typing before. I would be grateful if you would advise me if there are any suitable courses I could apply for, and the dates of the courses. I would be grateful if you would also send me details of accommodation for students.

I look forward to hearing from you.

Yours faithfully,
(sign your name)

Practice 27
   1 three
   2 look after Charmian and general light duties in the house
   3 near the park and a language school
   4 no, she will share until January, after that she will have her own room

Practice 28 Example answers:
   1 I am very interested in the theatre and music and I look forward to seeing some English plays.
   2 I am sure I will be able to learn about lots of interesting things with your daughter and I would like to learn karate myself.
   3 I am really looking forward to seeing the English countryside.
   4 I play a lot of tennis and I am glad I shall be able to practise with someone.
   5 I am very interested in the history of London and look forward to seeing all the famous sights.
   6 I am quite used to looking after young babies because I often take care of my sister's 3 month-old baby.

Practice 29   Example answer:
I would be grateful if you would register my name for Pottery classes on Monday evenings.

Practice 33   Example answer:
Dear Mrs Holdway,
Thank you for your letter. I have pleasure in accepting the position of au pair with your family.

I have several younger brothers and sisters and I am sure I will enjoy looking after your children, especially the baby!

I would like to attend English classes on one of my free evenings and I would be grateful if you would register my name.

I will arrive at the London air terminal on Saturday, July 22nd at 18.00hrs.; my flight is BA 632.

I think you will recognize me because I am very tall and I have long blond hair. I will also be carrying a red handbag. I am enclosing a recent photograph.

I am looking forward to meeting you next month.

Yours sincerely,
(sign your name)

Practice 34   1   Dear Y,
Thank you for the offer of a provisional place at the University, which I have pleasure in accepting.

I will send you confirmation of my degree results as soon as they are available.

Yours sincerely,
(sign your name)

2   Dear Y,
Thank you for your letter. I have pleasure in accepting the offer of a place on the 1st year Foundation course in Business Studies and Overseas Marketing.

I am enclosing a registration fee of £10 in an International Money Order.

I look forward to receiving any further details of the course.

Yours sincerely,
(sign your name)

Key

Practice 35 Example answers:
1 Dear Y,
Thank you for your letter. I am afraid that I do not wish to accept the offer as I would rather have a single room.

Yours sincerely,
(sign your name)

2 Dear Y,
Thank you for your letter. I am afraid I am unable to accept as I have already found a suitable position.

Yours sincerely,
(sign your name)

Practice 36 1 Dear Sir,
I would be grateful if you would send me two shoulder bags, one in pink and one in red.

I am enclosing a cheque for £8.

Yours faithfully,
(sign your name)

2 Dear Sir,
I would be grateful if you would send me a list of your secondhand records.

I am enclosing three International Reply Coupons.

Yours faithfully,
(sign your name)

Practice 37 1 Dear Sirs,
I am going to England next month to work as an au pair and I would be grateful if you could arrange overnight accommodation for me when I arrive.

I will be travelling on flight MAS 263 which arrives at the London air terminal on Tuesday August 10th at 19.00hrs. I plan to travel to my host family the next day.

Thank you for your help.

Yours faithfully,
(sign your name)

2 Dear Sir,
I have been accepted at a college in London as a full-time student and I would like to reserve a single room at your hostel if possible for ten months from October 1980.

I look forward to hearing from you with further details if there is a room available.

Yours faithfully,
(sign your name)

3 Dear Sir,
I would be grateful if you would send me one red T-shirt, medium size.

I enclose a p.o. value £2.50.

Yours faithfully,
(sign your name)

4 Dear Sir,
I would be grateful if you would send me a copy of the booklet 'London for Visitors'.

I am enclosing a p.o. for 50p and a sae.

Yours faithfully,
(sign your name)

5 Dear Sir,
I would like to book a place on the Intensive English Language course for Technical Students beginning on May 4th. I am enclosing a cheque for the deposit of £10.

I will require accommodation during the course and I would be grateful if you would send me details. I am willing to share.

Yours faithfully,
(sign your name)

Practice 38
1 to change her host family
2 she has too much work to do
3 South of England, not London
4 April

Practice 39
1 Although the family is kind, I do not have enough food.
2 Although I have plenty of food, the family is not very friendly.
3 Although I have lots of free time, I have to share a room.
4 Although it is a nice family, I am not used to looking after a very young baby.
5 Although the surroundings are pleasant, I do not get enough chance to practise my English because the family uses two languages. My hostess is German.

Practice 40
1 I would be grateful if you could forward my suitcase from the airport.
2 I would be grateful if you could re-address my letters to my current address.
3 I would be grateful if you could change this sweater for one of a larger size.

4   I would be grateful if you could send me a free sample of perfume.
5   I would be grateful if you could give me Tony's new address.

Practice 41

'Lane End,'
Casterton,
Carnforth,
Lancs.

HELP Agency,
72 High Street,
Acton,
London W3A 6AR

Dear Madam,
I am writing to ask if it is possible to work with another family.

Although I like the family and the village, there is no language school near here and I would like to practise my English more.

I would be grateful if you could place me with another family in a larger town. I would like to be near my friend Helga Spohn, who also works for your agency.

I look forward to hearing from you.

Yours faithfully,
  Michelle Munich

Practice 42   Example answers:
1   Dear Dr Craig,
    I am a student in the Pre-Proficiency class. I have spoken to my teacher about changing to a Proficiency class because the class I am studying in is too easy for me.

    I would be grateful if you would agree to the change.

    Yours sincerely,
    (sign your name)

2   Dear Mr Tibbetts,
    I am a student in Accountancy. I have spoken to my tutor, Mr Hamer, because I would like to study Economics instead.

    I would like to make an appointment to see you to discuss the matter.

    Yours sincerely,
    (sign your name)

3 Dear Miss Carter,
   I am a student in a Tuesday morning EFL class. I have talked to
   my class teacher because I would like to study in the evenings
   instead.

   I would be grateful if you would approve this change.

   Yours sincerely,
   (sign your name)

Practice 43 1 I would be grateful if you would replace this record because it is
   scratched.
2 I would be grateful if you would make the following corrections
   to my driving licence.
3 I would be grateful if you would refund my money because
   several pages of this book have been printed twice.
4 I would be grateful if you would arrange to collect the set of
   records I had on free trial because I do not wish to buy them.
5 I would be grateful if you would cancel my holiday booking and
   return my deposit.

Practice 44 Example answers:
1 Dear Sir,
   I wrote to you some time ago to ask about museums and special
   exhibitions at Easter in London, but I have not received a reply.
   I would be grateful if you would give me these details as soon as
   possible.

   Yours faithfully,
   (sign your name)

2 Dear Sir,
   I wrote to you three weeks ago to order a copy of the booklet
   'London for Visitors', but the booklet has still not arrived.

   I would be grateful if you would let me know if you received my
   letter and the enclosed p.o. for 50p.

   Yours faithfully,
   (sign your name)

3 Dear Sir,
   I wrote to you some time ago for the free brochures about your
   new sports car. I have not received a reply and I would be
   grateful if you would send me the brochures as soon as possible.

   Yours faithfully,
   (sign your name)

4 Dear Sir,
   I wrote to you some time ago about a performance of a ballet
   which was changed at the last minute. I have not received a

reply to my letter and I would be grateful if you would either
refund my money or send tickets for the ballet that was
advertised ('Swan Lake').

Yours faithfully,
(sign your name)

Practice 45   1   You do not need to write a letter, you can ring up.
2   You do not need to write a letter, you can ring up to confirm the
appointment, but if you live too far away, you could write a
short letter.
3   You need to write a letter.

Practice 46   1   F107183
2   The Under Secretary of State
3   Home Office,
Lunar House,
Wellesley Road,
CROYDON, CR9 2BY
4a   letter from his college
4b   bank statement or similar
4c   passport

Practice 47   1   He is writing because Ahmad has not attended several lectures
and tutorials.
2   He must go and see Mr Roxbee

Practice 48   1   I am writing to apologize for my account being overdrawn. I'm
afraid the monthly money from my parents has not arrived yet,
but I will soon have additional funds credited to my account.
2   I am writing to apologize for missing my appointment but I am
afraid I made a mistake with the dates. I would be grateful if I
could make another appointment.
3   I am writing to apologize for missing the oral exam. I am afraid I
overslept. I hope it is possible to retake the exam at a later date.

Practice 49   1   I'm sorry I haven't written for such a long time but I've been ill.
2   I'm sorry I haven't written for so long but I've been studying for
exams.
3   I'm sorry I haven't written for such a long time but I've been
very busy.

Practice 51   Example answers:
1   I've been reading a lot of difficult books for my course and
gambling too much at night.

2 I've been looking after the children during the day and going out at night to a good new club with my friends.

3 I went to a film yesterday and I've been planning a tour of England during the summer.

4 I have enrolled in a Pottery class and I met an interesting Greek boy in the class.

5 I have been working hard but also going to a lot of parties because it's Christmas.

6 I've been feeling rather ill so I've been watching a lot of television.

7 I've been losing weight because I've been eating healthy food.

8 I've been going out a lot with a new girlfriend and spending a lot of money.

Practice 52 Example Answer for question 6.
I've been feeling rather ill so I've been staying at home and watching a lot of television. I think I like the children's programmes best, as they aren't full of gun fights!

Practice 53 Example answers:

1	upset	6	happy
2	annoyed	7	embarrassed
3	thrilled	8	sad
4	pleased	9	interested
5	excited	10	tired

Practice 54 Example answer:
— sorry I haven't written for a long time
— How are you?
— last month I moved house
— { I was very upset
    It was very embarrassing

Practice 61 Example answers:
1   your home address

Dear Miss Ayton,
I was a student in your class last year and I am writing to ask you for a short reference and a certificate of attendance because I hope to attend classes here.

Thank you for your help.

Yours sincerely,
   Helga Spohn

2 Dear Madam,
   I was a student in English at the College last year and I would
   like to write to some friends in my class, but I do not have their
   addresses. I would be very grateful if you could give me the
   address of these two people;
   Marie Scarpato
   Karin Labbi

   Thank you very much for your help.

   Yours sincerely,

Note You probably know this person, but you might not be able to
remember their name. In this case you can end 'sincerely'.

3   your home address

   Dear Mrs Pye,
   I am writing because I don't think I remembered to give you my
   home address before I left England. I'd be very grateful if you
   could send on any mail that has arrived for me.

   Best wishes,
   (sign your name)

4   your home address

   Dear Mr Blake,
   I was a student at the hostel last year, in Room 64, and I would
   be grateful if you could let me know if the gold pen I lost has
   been found yet. If it has, could you please send it to the above
   address.

   Thank you for your help.

   Yours sincerely,
   (sign your name)

Practice 62 1 I have an account etc
                 2 . . . I have now returned . . . etc
                 3 . . . if you would arrange . . . etc
                 4 Thank you for . . . etc

Practice 63 Example answers:
                 1 I'd be very grateful if you could look for a blue silk shirt which I
                    think I must have left in my room. If you find it, could you send
                    it to me please and I will send you the cost of the postage
                    immediately.
                 2 Can you do me a favour? Can you send me the latest Led
                    Zeppelin L.P? Let me know if there is anything from here you'd
                    like in return.

3 I'd like to ask you a favour. My slides should arrive soon and I'd
   be very grateful if you would send them on to me. I am
   enclosing a money order to cover the cost of the postage.
4 Do you think you could buy me another set of slides of Oxford –
   mine were no good! Of course I'll pay you for them.
5 Can I ask you a favour? Can you ask at Mothercare if they could
   send their catalogue direct to me?

Practice 64 Example answer:
1 Dear Michelle,
   Well – I'm back home at last. I caught the boat train you told me
   about and had a terrible trip across the channel. Everyone was
   sick except two old drunks who held onto their whisky in the
   bar. I stayed with Pierre and Jean in Paris-remember them?
   They always talked too much in class and they still do, but we
   had a good time. Again I was a bit ill because of the food. It was
   SO delicious and I've put on two kilos AT LEAST. When I got
   home they had a party for me – it was good at first to see
   everyone again but nothing has changed at all. The biggest
   excitement of the week was my sister's new haircut and her new
   boyfriend (who is as thick as a plank).

   Of course I had to start work after a few days – in a Chemical
   factory. Its alright I suppose but I miss my freedom in England.
   I'm already thinking of leaving again and going to America, but
   I daren't tell my parents. My mother already has plans for
   marrying me off to someone here. So I'm saving money madly
   (the job is boring but well paid) and hope to go to the States
   next year. You must come and see me if your're having a
   continental holiday this year. I may have gone mad by then –
   but COME.

   love
     Helga

2 Dear Thomas,
   I'm really fed-up. I've been back in Switzerland for three months
   and STILL haven't got a job. Its very depressing especially as I
   thought that my degree was good enough, but there are lots of
   us with good degrees. There just aren't enough jobs to go round.
   I knew that I would be a bit depressed at leaving England
   because Cathy couldn't come with me, but living at home again
   is strange. My parents still think of me as the little boy who
   went away from home so my mother keeps cooking, and my
   father keeps asking me what I'm going to do. It is all a bit
   stifling. They're very kind but . . . Anyway, what chance of a
   job with your firm? Are there any jobs in my area? PLEASE

write soon and tell me – I expect that its the same in England – but at least I could see Cathy again. If I don't go back to England soon I think she may come in her holidays. And that will be a problem with my parents.

Sorry about sounding so miserable – but I am.

Peter

Practice 65 Example answers:
1 Dear X,
I am a friend of David's and he suggested I might be able to stay with you for a few days on my way back home. I'd be very grateful if I could and it's not too much trouble. I don't know the city at all so I'd be grateful if you could tell me how to get to your house from the station.

Many thanks,
(sign you name)

2 Dear X,
I have come to study in Britain and my parents have asked me to bring a parcel for you. Would you like me to post it to you? If it's more convenient I could deliver it myself.

I don't know much about Britain yet, so I'd be grateful if you could tell me how to find your house.

Yours sincerely,
(sign your name)

Practice 66 1 ~~The~~ life hasn't changed in ~~this~~ village. ~~It's~~ very peaceful. ~~I'm~~ returning by bus next week, ~~is it~~ possible ~~for you to~~ meet me at ~~the~~ station?
2 ~~We have~~ just arrived ~~here. The~~ weather ~~is~~ very warm. ~~I've~~ still got ~~a~~ dreadful cold. Brian ~~is~~ fine ~~and we~~ both send ~~our~~ love ~~to you.~~

Practice 67 Example answer:
1 Saw Liz last week, much fatter than at Christmas. She wants to stay another year because of the good food!
2 The weather isn't good, but going on a boat trip tomorrow. Wish you were here. See you next week.

Practice 68 Example answers:
1 This is a sentry on duty outside Buckingham Palace.
2 I have swum in the sea!
3 This is the cable-car we could see from our room.

Practice 69   Example answers:
1   It's raining of course.
2   It's too hot to lie on the beach.
3   It's not cold when you're skiing.

Practice 71   1   e   4   b
2   d   5   a
3   c

Practice 72   Example answers:
1   Called round to return record but no answer. Didn't want to leave it outside, so phone when you get back and I'll bring it round. Let's eat out tonight.
2   Dear Mrs Fiddick,
Some friends called unexpectedly to take me out to eat, so I won't be home for supper. Could you leave a key please as I will be late. Sorry if this causes you any trouble.
3   Thanks for the book. I loved it and it made me think.
4   Milkman, please leave 3 extra pints and a small single cream Monday. Thanks.
5   Johnny, Patricia 'phoned. Please phone her – before 9pm at Julie's place.

Practice 73   1   Dear Mrs Gibbs,
Thank you very much for the book. It is a lovely gift and I shall always be reminded of England when I read it.

Again, many thanks,

Yours sincerely,
(sign your name)

2   Dear Mr Isaacs,

Thank you very much for the delicious meal. We all enjoyed ourselves very much and learnt a lot of new English words!

Yours,
(sign your name)